"A visionary book grounded in experiential wisdom. Brandon and Venneikia share the architecture of spiritual community that will inspire and guide any leader eager to build circles of belonging and becoming. Where these folks are leading, we are lucky to follow."

—CASPER TER KUILE
Cofounder, Sacred Design Lab

"There are tons of books on church innovation. *Liberating Church* is one of the first to center Black religious experience. The faith communities profiled here remind us that God is indeed doing a new thing. If we move past our preconceptions and listen carefully, we just might recognize it."

—CHANEQUA WALKER-BARNES
Columbia Theological Seminary

"*Liberating Church* is not a book for those playing church or who are in denial of its complicated histories. It is a prophetic text grounding itself in the wisdom of the past in order to call contemporary Christians to reorient their lives and faith practices. The words found in these pages will feel like fresh air for those seeking to honor God, others, their ancestors, and themselves through truth telling, justice seeking, and community building."

—ALICIA CROSBY
Justice educator, equity consultant, and minister

"The doors to the church did not just close when the pandemic began. Those of us who are queer or trans/nonbinary, or disabled, or poor know all too well what it means to be shut out from what is supposed to be life-giving, not death dealing. *Liberating Church* offers a powerful framework for change, breathing the spirit of the hush harbors into a new season of possibility, innovation, accountability, and care, particularly for the Black church."

—MYKAL O. SLACK

Community minister, Black Lives of Unitarian Universalism

"This book is a treasure in bringing the mission of the church and the work of social justice together to learn from the Black folk theology and revolutionary practice of enslaved Africans. . . . This book is required reading for anyone who wants to see the church be different, be community, be an agent of change. Get your copy and, more importantly, put the wisdom in these pages into practice in your life, ministry, and activism!"

—BILLY MICHAEL HONOR

Community organizer, public scholar, and former church planter

Liberating Church

VOICES

The Voices Project gathers leaders of color who influence culture (the church, education, the arts, politics, media, and business) for important conversations, challenges, and triumphs within communities of color and roles as cultural influencers.

The Voices series is a vehicle by which we join the rich literary heritage of BIPOC (Black, Indigenous People of Color) writers, a history that is rich but still lags in the larger context of publishing. There simply are not enough writers of color. This collection of work will close that gap, offering insights, inspiration, and a unique cultural worldview that will impact life and culture in translucent ways that shine a beacon towards a flourishing society. The voices in this series will move us closer to Shalom as did their ancestors.

The Voices Project
PO Box 16367
Portland, OR 97292

twitter.com/jointhevoices
facebook.com/jointhevoices
instagram.com/jointhevoices

Liberating Church

A Twenty-First Century
Hush Harbor Manifesto

EDITED BY
Brandon Wrencher
AND Venneikia Samantha Williams

FOREWORD BY
Lynice Pinkard

CASCADE *Books* • Eugene, Oregon

LIBERATING CHURCH
A Twenty-First Century Hush Harbor Manifesto

Cascade Books
An Imprint of Wipf and Stock Publishers
199 W. 8th Ave., Suite 3
Eugene, OR 97401

www.wipfandstock.com

PAPERBACK ISBN: 978-1-6667-3004-3
HARDCOVER ISBN: 978-1-6667-2106-5
EBOOK ISBN: 978-1-6667-2107-2

Cataloguing-in-Publication data:

Names: Wrencher, Brandon, editor. | Williams, Venneikia Samantha, editor. | Pinkard, Lynice, foreword.

Title: Liberating church : a twenty-first-century hush harbor manifesto / edited by Brandon Wrencher and Venneikia Samantha Williams ; foreword by Lynice Pinkard.

Description: Eugene, OR : Cascade Books, 2022 | Voices | Includes bibliographical references.

Identifiers: ISBN 978-1-6667-3004-3 (paperback) | ISBN 978-1-6667-2106-5 (hardcover) | ISBN 978-1-6667-2107-2 (ebook)

Subjects: LCSH: Freedom (Theology). | Liberation theology. | Church renewal.

Classification: BT810.2 .L53 2022 (paperback) | BT810.2 .L53 (ebook)

VERSION NUMBER 040522

Contents

Foreword

THIS BOOK IS A clarion call and a summons to alternative, countercultural forms of community, a way of doing and being church that is both ancient and new.

For me, and for the writers who drafted these pages, churches exist only to serve people and planet. The church is not an empire, a way for leaders to build monuments to themselves, for congregants to take pride in the curb appeal that a "lovely edifice" affords. The church is not a building. (God has left the building!) The church is not "professional holy people" that keep things running, or personalities that fill up mega-stadiums, or charisma with no character, or gifts without fruit—none of that.

The church is an extension of Christ—literally Christ's body—called to be an alternative to the militaristic, well-defended, consumerist, alienated way of life that is the norm—a way of life built on coercion, competition, or collective self-interest—and to incarnate newness in the service of the flourishing of all life.

We are honestly being called to abandon, to disengage from, to desert the American systems of death into which we have been inculcated—to break the hold that these death systems have on us. We are being called to put aside the bad news of the world and all of its organized systems of destruction, to walk away from the zombie death march, to put aside the dominant, dehumanizing values that are all around us—white supremacy, vulture capitalism, queer- and trans-hatred, Christian hegemony, oppression, and abuse of every kind. A life-sucking, death-dealing system cannot be reformed in the name of progress, no matter whose politics rule the day. These writers understand that all the walls are falling down and have ceased trying to prop them up. We are being called by the Spirit of Life to GET OUT! We are being called off the plantation and into the hush harbor. I hear the Spirit saying, let this murderous and anti-creation system collapse in the world as well as in you.

This book and the ecclesial experiments it describes urge us to disengage from the postures, habits, and assumptions that define the world of power and injustice that is so devoid of mercy and compassion. The call is away from ordinary life, ordinary possessions, and ordinary assumptions, to a way of life that the dominant culture—the death culture—judges to be impossible. Thus, we are being called to be something that by logic and reason and sheer effort is indeed impossible. (Remember that what is constructed on the basis of effort always ends up collapsing from exhaustion.)

But effort is not all we have, and that is the miraculous reminder of this volume.

Inside us—by which I mean inside you, me, the writers of this book, their friends and accomplices—there lives something that the society that seeks to control us can never know or reach. This "something" is an inchoate, largely incoherent, and irrepressible energy that has demolished empires. This power cannot be fortressed, locked down, or held against its will. And it grows when we gather.

The God of Many Names calls all people into fullness of life in and through *community*. It is always about community because we are not individually salvageable. The call is not to join an institution or to sign a pledge card. The call is to sign on to a different account of reality that is in profound contrast to the dominant account of reality into which we have all been inducted. These writers move and excite me because they have accepted this call and are working to live into it.

Societies are never able to examine or overhaul themselves: this effort must be made by the fugitives, the disenchanted, the prophets that every society cunningly and unfailingly secretes.

(The Scripture calls these ones "yeast.") This ferment, this disturbance, is the responsibility and the necessity of the alternative communities described here.

It is important to note that our mission is dangerous. Our mission is risky, because God's will for the world is in deep tension with the way that the world is organized and also with how the church is typically organized. Institutional church programs and denominational structures are often too removed from real, radical (root) spirituality steeped in justice, instead becoming bulwarks against the movement of the Spirit and preserving old patterns of power ill-suited to the real message of our faith.

The American churches, with far too few exceptions, do not produce people who are more fully alive, who are able to bear and speak truth, or who are growing steadily toward wholeness and liberation. More and more, "church people" have settled for fanciful forms of personal piety and for promises of personal prosperity. We do not want to admit this, and we do not admit it. We are very cruelly trapped between what we say we would like to be and what we refuse to say we actually are. And we cannot possibly become what we would like to be until we are able to ask ourselves why the lives that so many "believers" lead in this country are mainly so empty, so tame, and so small. Inured to the reality of global corporate empire-building and its parasitical processes, the church simply has no reason to revolt. Instead, the church, like the consumer-capitalist culture shot all through it, is fixated on "good marketing strategies" and "unlimited growth," the net effect of which is to keep people at a safe remove from the radically transformative experience of the gospel. Consequently, our "religion" cannot possibly fulfill its original function of disturbing the peace.

Moreover, our mission is profoundly conflictual because the dissident disciples in hush harbor communities love and are committed to the freedom of those who have been targeted—the sick (all forms of sickness), the dying (by virus or violence), the poor, the oppressed, the captives (imprisoned in every sense of the word), the devastated, the homicidal, the suicidal, the addict, the children.

The present system works as it does precisely because a certain "quota" of lives have been "handed over" to anti-human (and yes, anti-Black) forces, and the systems prosper on their backs. The attempt to draw those "handed over" back into the realm of love and forgiveness and compassion and generosity and solidarity will evoke deep hostility in the death system. The normal state of the fugitive is to be in trouble with the authorities, who are characteristically defenders of the systems that deny humanness. This is why we have to learn to speak treason fluently because we are being called to speak words beyond our capacity in the face (to the face) of "the powers that be."

In connection with these writers' important provocations, I feel compelled to speak a word of love to the Black church. The very *necessity* of hush harbors corroborates that being Black in America has always been about surviving our own murder. It must be understood that hush harbors exist largely outside the bounds of churches, including Black churches.

Notwithstanding the richness of the Black freedom struggle, the Black church, by which I mean the vast majority of churchgoing Black people who belong to one of the eight Black-controlled religious organizations founded by Black people for Black people, constitute a significant component in the larger matrix of domination.

Even in instances in which Black religious leaders, congregations, or denominations engage in social activism, their protest is framed in such a way that the basic structure of American capitalism remains unchallenged. Also, while those religiously inspired protest efforts express vehement opposition to racism, they generally ignore the intricate relationships between the overarching forms of domination that constitute the American Empire (racism, capitalism, sexism), its derivatives (heterosexism, homophobia, transphobia), and all of the other organized systems of destruction, including warmongering and ecological devastation.

My criticism of "the church" in the American context does not mean to imply that there are no revolutionary acts of resistance by individual churches, church members, or church leaders.

I am writing as a Black, lesbian pastor, and the Black church is my home, but when I was still a very young girl, for reasons that I could not explain to myself or to others, I suddenly felt that I did not belong anywhere. As it turned out, my sexuality was the least of it. One minute, I was content in my family, my church, my choir, my youth group, and the next, in other people's eyes, indeed, in my own, I was moving, inexorably, to the edge of the world.

At the edges, in these very communities that reject the limits imposed by existing institutions and imaginaries, I have found other fugitives, exiles become witnesses, singing an unfinished abolitionist anthem, living an exodus both archive and prophecy, who look out at the desiccated world and shout, "No!"

These writers understand that life happens at the edges. We believe that faith is aligned with the absurd, the incommunicable, and the extraordinary embedded in ordinary life. Exodus is in fact evidence of sacred futures. The writers of this book are determined to conspire with alternatives, to be the midwives that will let the babies live, the artisans who will fashion the baskets, a people living into the eschatological truth of our always-already freedom.

To be called out is a countercultural summons; to be sent back in is a countercultural practice. It is a two-way deal. We are always called to *disengage* death systems and the death culture and to *embrace* people and planet so as to work with God (Love) to co-create more aliveness and flourishing.

It is time to go out, to go back in. It is time to go in, in order to get others out.

There is a plaintive refrain rising over the fields, and it is time to move. With this book, you hold in your hands a forged traveling pass; a worn, often-folded map passed hand to hand by those who, like you, are headed north; a true compass that points toward freedom. I pray I will meet you there.

LYNICE PINKARD

Invocation

We remember the wisdom of Sojourner Truth.
"Truth is powerful and it prevails."
May integrity be the ground we stand on.

We remember the poetry of Art Blakey.
"Whatever truth drops on it eventually grinds to a powder."
May truth rise and fall, particles in the wind and breath.

We remember the fierceness of Nina Simone.
"I had spent many years pursuing excellence, because that is what classical music is all about . . . Now it was dedicated to freedom, and that was far more important."
May fierceness fuel our flame.

We remember the vigilance of Malcolm X.
"You can't separate peace from freedom because no one can be at peace unless he has his freedom."
May vigilance be our flint.

We remember the perseverance of Marsha P. Johnson.
"How many years has it taken people to realize that we are all brothers and sisters and human beings in the human race?"
May the human struggle be heard in the rustling of the tree limbs, never deaf in our ears.

We remember the vibrant imagination of Octavia Butler.
"I recognize we will pay more attention when we have different leadership."
May creativity stir us to dream.

We remember the discipline of Septima Poinsette Clark.
"I believe unconditionally in the ability of people to respond when they are told the truth. We need to be taught to study rather than believe, to inquire rather than to affirm."
May we engage the Holy text with rigor and expectancy.

We remember the steadfastness of Fannie Lou Hamer.
"Sometimes it seem like to tell the truth today is to run the risk of being killed. But if I fall, I'll fall five feet four inches forward in the fight for freedom."
May our eyes be fixed on freedom.

We remember the accuracy of Ella Baker.
"In order for us as poor and oppressed people to become part of a society that is meaningful, the system under which we now exist has to be radically changed. . . It means facing a system that does not lend itself to your needs and devising means by which you change that system."
May justice drive out all that harms.

We remember the depth of great joy of Mahalia Jackson.
"How can you sing of amazing grace and all God's wonders without using your hands?"
May the joy of God take shape in our body, our actions.

Hush Harbor

Come and Get Free

The stars light the sky.
They show us the way.
Together, with the ancestors, we are here.
The trees surround us.
Our space is protected.
The ground is consecrated.
A place is prepared.
The lamp is lit.
The Holy Text is speaking.
Truth-shouts shatter all lies.
Our eyes are opened.
Justice takes shape.
Joy stamps out fear.
We are free.

Acknowledgments

THIS BOOK IS DEDICATED to the ancestors of the hush harbors of old, and all of those who by the liberating and risky power of the Spirit are creating modern hush harbors that are alternatives to the church-industrial complex,[1] especially to the six faith communities lifted up in this book. We give thanks to the Louisville Institute for their generous financial and networking support through the Pastoral Study Research Grant. We give thanks to our teachers and guides—those who are still with us in the flesh: Rev. Dr. Katie Day, Rev. Dr. Stephen G. Ray, Rev. Lynice Pinkard, Rev. Dr. Nelson Johnson, Rev. Dr. Alexia Salvatierra, and Bishop Tonyia Rawls. You have provided us your mentorship, technical assistance, teaching and training, prayers, blessing, and most importantly, your example. We must give a special note of appreciation to the late Dr. Albert J. Raboteau, one of the chief religious historians of the hush harbors and Black religion. Dr. Raboteau was a pilot light for us and gave his blessing to our work in 2019. And we give thanks for those other teachers and guides who have moved on to be with the eternal cloud of witnesses that are too numerous to name. We extend a huge debt of gratitude to Symone Williams, who served as our research assistant. Symone joined our team in the summer of 2020 to help us move to the next leg of the race at the beginning of the coronavirus global pandemic when we were all dealing with so much fatigue and loss. Thank you to Karen

---

1. Dan White and J. R. Woodward use the phrase "church as industrial complex" in their book, *The Church as Movement*.

Archia for a brilliant book cover design that reflects the shades and textures of Black people! We could not do this work without the support of our spouses, families, and communities. You have cheered us on, reviewed our writing in the late night hours, held down the home front when we were away at writing retreats, and so much more. We are, because of your love and support for us! Finally, we acknowledge and summon future generations, those prophetic leaders to come, to learn from and remix our witness for innovating your own hush harbors for Black futures unseen. We write this to and for you and honor you!

Introduction

The Journey Ahead

THANK YOU FOR ENTERING this journey with us into the ancient and present portal of the hush harbors. The seeds of *Liberating Church* began in 2016 at a retreat at the historic Highlander Research and Education Center in Tennessee, when Anthony Smith and I (Brandon) with other Black clergy activist friends were grappling with deep questions of belonging and becoming. How do we serve the prophetic call of Jesus' ministry and teaching in a time when churches are so often not serving the deepest spiritual and social challenges of our time? Instead, we see a proliferation of churches that are well adjusted to the status quo of terror and misery, even, and especially, when it is represented by Black faces in high places. Since this assimilationist model of church is so widespread, those of us who seek a different way are a remnant. How do we not go this prophetic path alone, given the overwhelming lack of support for this type of prophetic-pastoral leadership by denominations and local churches? Congregations are often not places where we feel we can be brave and authentic.

We confessed that our activism and organizing in the local community often opened transformations for us that our congregations did not, that the local movement was functioning as sacred space for us and for many of our unchurched activist comrades. These sacred movement spaces were hidden in plain sight, off the grid from our religious structures. What is the cost of waiting to turn around established churches to embody the prophetic call given the fierce urgency of so many justice and healing issues? Is our only option to wait for vacancies in those few revered prophetic pulpits that have stood the test of time? Do we start new faith communities? Embracing our need for wisdom, we looked back into the history of the Black religious experience. When did Black folks catalyze collective, spiritually rooted, revolutionary action in the world without widespread institutional support and political power? The civil rights movement was an obvious place to turn. But we each had to acknowledge the limits to the civil rights model of male, clerical, Southern respectable, Christian prophetic witness. Similar limits existed for the abolitionist movement and concurrent protests that led to Black independent denominations. In this age of the Black Lives Matter movement, Black women, queer folk, hip hop, and folk religion are at the center of Black-led, spiritually rooted struggles for justice. We needed to go to a different place to glean wisdom for this moment. We turned to the antebellum hush harbors, covert spaces of worship and activism where Black people did not need to enter by showing their assimilation to white, Christian, patriarchal, and capitalist ways of being. These conversations led to me (Brandon) pulling together a team of clergy activists from across the United States to engage in research on a few key questions. As the North American church grapples with an eroding position of privilege in society, what is a decolonizing vision of church from the margins? In what ways did the antebellum hush harbors function as expressions of church? Where are the contemporary hush harbors within the US?

As a team of faith-rooted activists, we began our research through engaging in literature reviews of both hush harbors and decolonial theory. Through these reviews, eight guiding marks of a liberating church were created: Steal Away, North Star, Ubuntu, All God's Children Got Shoes, Talking Book, Sankofa, Joy Unspeakable, and Stay Woke. The eight marks are a guide towards a decolonial framework of spiritual activism and liberative gathering.

Steal Away orients us towards fugitivity, an attitude necessary for entering into the consciousness of both hush harbors and a liberating church. With this fugitive orientation, we are guided by North Star to begin the work of imagining and build-ing a new world, one that is "present, but not yet." Ubuntu centers interdependence, acknowledging the abundance that springs forth through collective faith, trust, and intimacy. Alongside interde-pendence, All God's Children Got Shoes centers collaborative and equitable leadership structures, affirming the dignity of all folks to lead and be leader-full. Talking Book asks us to diligently question which Jesus and which Bible we are choosing to follow, emphasizing that only a certain Jesus and a specific Bible will route us to actualizing freedom into the present. Sankofa reminds us to balance as we look back to foster our rich ancestral roots, taking with us what is necessary while looking forward to harvesting seeds for the future. With balance, Joy Unspeakable necessitates a radical love plus deep healing that transforms transgenerational wounds, allowing for an unspeakable, liberating transcension that only the somatic expression of joy captures. And lastly, Stay Woke grounds us in the wake of the afterlife of slavery, challenging us to re-membering and re-memory as we embody the consciousness of the hush harbors in ever-changing landscapes and conditions.

Our team then engaged in ethnographic research at six min-istries in Black communities in the South. We used the eight marks as a methodology to shape our ethnographic tools that included interviews with clergy and lay leaders and a survey distributed to the membership of each community. The six communities were: The Gathering (Dallas, TX), Good Neighbor Movement (Greens-boro, NC), Greenway Community (Winston-Salem, NC), Mission House (Salisbury, NC), New Birth Community AME Church (Greensboro, NC), and QC Family Tree (Charlotte, NC). Four of the six communities are led by members of the research team. No team member was involved in researching the community they lead. Each of these ministry sites are less than twenty years old, in Black communities, prioritize blackness and celebrate Black cul-ture, history, and ancestors. These spiritual communities actively better the lives of their wider community through art and cultural opportunities, educational support, providing community meals, sheltering unhoused folks, and advocating for policy change.

Following the site visits to each community, the research team engaged in qualitative and quantitative analysis of the interviews and surveys, as the eight marks were represented in convergent and divergent ways within each and across all of the communities. Not only are the eight marks present in each of these six communities, but each of these communities are models of a contemporary liberating church.

Surely, there are constellations of contemporary hush harbors that we have yet to know, and others that are soon to come. The goal of Liberating Church is to work to build a network of communities that exemplify the structural critique and spiritual power of the hush harbors. Womanist thinkers and religious historians have written about the revolutionary nature of the hush harbors. We build on their legacy to articulate the practical potential of hush harbors, to write a hush-harbor ecclesiology. What the Spirit started in the hush harbors continues still.

In the pages that follow, you will encounter the practices and principles of six young Black-centered spiritual communities interpreted through the eight marks of Liberating Church. The book starts with a couple of chapters ("A Changing Landscape" and "Church from the Margins") that further sets the context for why we need Liberating Church. The book then shifts to eight chapters that describe the eight marks of a Liberating Church. Each chapter begins with quotes that reflect the mark, followed by an essay that dances back and forth between the historical and present portal of the hush harbors. The book then shifts to introduce the six communities, giving a brief snapshot of each community's context, mission, impact, and how they align with the eight marks of Liberating Church. We conclude the book sharing our comparative analysis of the marks across the six communities and encouragement to continue the tradition of the hush harbors. A litany of prayerful intentions transitions the conclusion to several back-matter pieces. First, we include an epilogue that is a love note to future generations that carry the hush harbor movement forward in creative ways. We write this letter seeking to be holy and good ancestors now to those who follow in our wake. Following the epilogue, we include data from our ethnographic research. We believe that data gives sound basis for the bold witness and stark changes we advocate for in this book. We include reflection questions for readers to grapple with, enter into conversation with others about, and use as a way to experiment with the practices and principles in the book. Finally, we close with the bios of contributors and a bibliography.

We want to say a word about the title. Why did we choose *liberating* over *liberated* church? The hush harbors were *portable* sites of the sacred and revolutionary. They were not arrivals, destinations, accomplishments. Hush harbors are sites of becoming, process ecclesiologies. Likewise, through this book we call forth churches engaged in liberat*ing* work, because no one is liberated until all people and the planet have been set free. The title has another meaning, though. We don't only call forth liberation in the society, but also in the church. The hush harbors set enslaved Africans free from the assimilationist and supremacist ways that plantation churches gathered. We hope this book will inspire the liberating of church as we have come to know it in our time and the future. That our reflections on the witness and power of the antebellum hush harbors and these six faith communities will serve as a manifesto, a public declaration, a call to action, a revolutionary decree to completely undo the church-industrial complex, and to build a movement of liberating churches.

Liberating Church: A Twenty-First Century Hush Harbor Manifesto is written as a tool for ministry leaders and faith-rooted activists, those with formal education and those trained by the wisdom of struggling in the streets. We write this book first for the Black diaspora, specifically to: Black genderqueer folk, Black church wanderers (those whose culture is the Black church but who no longer find that space as home), Black activists, organizers, and social entrepreneurs, Black church planters, and Black e(x)vangelicals. We also write more broadly to all activists, faith leaders, church planters, practical theologians, religious educators, and everyday neighborhood leaders who care about building a better world and believe churches should help midwife that world.

We kept the book short in length to be more of a toolkit, to be used in small groups, in classrooms, in trainings and teach-ins, and in sermon series, among ministry professionals with laity, among professional organizers and activists with the neighbors they bring together. You will find lots of tools throughout these pages to assist your conversations and strategizing: discussion questions, data, illustrations, anecdotes, practices, and more. May this book be a resource that stirs good trouble and revolutionary practice within your community!

A Changing Landscape

Time is filled with swift transition
Naught of earth unmoved can stand
Build your hopes on things eternal
Hold to God's unchanging hand[1]

DECEMBER 31, 2019, MANY a preacher spent their Watch Night services speaking of the Church's need for "20/20 vision." Congregants were told that 2020 was the year of clearer sight and God's plans being fully revealed. The apostle Paul tells us that we both know and prophesy in part, and these statements were evidence of such. Though there was truth in the statement, how might it have been more rooted in the spirit of the age than the spirit of God?

So many of our pulpits and churches are deeply shaped by empire, individualism, capitalist consumption, and triumphalism. We could not perceive that 20/20 vision might mean the painful upending of individual idols and collective entanglements. In the year 2020, we grappled with the implications of what many have described as an *apocalyptic* moment. The COVID-19 pandemic is apocalyptic. It unmasks and lays bare the pre-existing conditions that have diseased the body politic of the United States for decades, even centuries. By *apocalyptic*, we do not speak of an escapist end-time theology that disciples people to await a rapture. We are using

1. J.B. Wilson, "Hold to God's Unchanging Hand."

"apocalypse" in the truest sense of the word, which is a rupture, an unmasking, and uncovering of the world that is.

As the year 2020 slowly unfolded before us, the Church, America, and most of its inhabitants were forced to see the world and our place in it with new eyes. Things that have long been true about the state of this nation were finally acknowledged as factual and not just a matter of opinion. The people of God were reminded that *they* are the Church, and not just the building they once gathered in before social distancing became the norm.

What now lies before the Church is an opportunity to repent, readjust, and reclaim the prophetic, radical strands that our ancestors modeled for us. The disruption of COVID-19 is a call into imaginative practices as seen in the antebellum hush harbors. In the words of writer Arundhati Roy, "The pandemic is a portal."[2] For enslaved Africans enduring the horrors of chattel slavery in the United States, the hush harbors were hidden portals and safe spaces for healing, connection, and liberation. Today, the hush harbors extend to us the same invitation, but we must have ears to hear and eyes to see the Spirit's call.

Too often churches, the preacher class, and others in the faith community have not stood firm in their position as the conscience of the state and have instead colluded with forces that trample the poor, the disabled, the sick, the outcast, the imprisoned, and the immigrant. The minor and major prophets of the Old Testament make clear God's grief and judgment for such collusion.

We can no longer put all our eggs in the basket of Sunday morning gatherings. The status quo has been disrupted. The cult of personality and the structures of hierarchy that order life together in churches are being exposed as insufficient for the times.

Said another way: this moment has revealed that the way we have organized churches produces consumers not disciples, acquaintances not deep friendships, behavior modification not deep repentance, and volun-tourists not liberationists, flag-wavers not cross bearers, concubines of the state and not its conscience.

2. Roy, "The Pandemic Is a Portal."

If the very existence of the Church is meant to be leaven in the dough, salt in the meal, and light for all those who dwell in the human household, then ecclesial community must accept the obligations that derive from its essential function.

—Juan Luis Segundo[3]

We are now forced to grapple with the need for egalitarian (often virtual) spaces rooted in mutuality. Now, more than ever, it seems we must make a radical turn. At our best, the Church brings unique gifts to this work. Think about it: we are a community of people who have been called into a life-long practice of repentance and transformation that demands that we face our frailties and faults while holding on to a sense of our belovedness. What would it look like for the church to be a leavening presence, aiding this work of transformation to take place on the personal, communal, and political levels of our cities and world?

Moving forward is a must.

Do not long for the captivity experienced in Egypt just because the unknown ahead is discomforting. The Spirit of God goes before us. Where the Spirit of God is, there is freedom. We are being presented with the opportunity to truly see abolition accomplished. For every way in which people are exploited, dehumanized, and discarded, we can now build structures in their stead where all can flourish and *shalom*, peace, can be felt.

We will not go back to normal. Normal never was. Our pre-Corona existence was not normal other than we normalized greed, inequity, exhaustion, depletion, extraction, disconnection, confusion, rage, hoarding, hate and lack. We should not long to return my friends. We are being given the opportunity to stitch a new garment. One that fits all of humanity and nature.[4]

Mary of Nazareth's Son once said, "you cannot put new wine into old wineskin." The new wine of revolutionary beloved

3. Segundo, *A Theology for Artisans of a New Humanity*, 81.

4. Sonya Renee Taylor (@sonyareneetaylor), Instagram photo, April 2, 2020, https://www.instagram.com/p/B-fc3ejAlvd/?hl=en.

community calls for new wineskin. Revolutionary oneness is not new; it is rooted in the ancient witness of Jesus of Nazareth and his prayerful vision of a new humanity and a new order arranged by love. We need only look to the antebellum hush harbors for Jesus' vision and new order in these yet to be United States of America.

Church from the Margins

*Reclaiming the inspiration and intention of our ancestors
who acknowledged the sacredness of the earth, its power
to stand as witness is vital to our contemporary survival.
Again and again in slave narratives we read about Black
folks taking to the hills in search of freedom, moving into
deep wilderness to share their sorrow with the natural hab-
itat. We read about ways they found solace in wild things.*

—bell hooks[1]

*The only church service I know any thing about was when
the slaves would get together once in awhile at night and
have prayer meetins and sing.*

—Stearlin Arwine, formerly enslaved African[2]

CHRISTIANITY IN THE UNITED States has not always been behold-
en to white supremacy. While the plantation church enforced chattel slavery through the racist prooftexting of biblical submission
narratives, another Christianity was being born in the antebellum
hush harbors. Rejecting the segregated rafters of Black-only balco-
nies, this church stole away to the wild places: the woods, swamps,
uninhabitable wastelands where the Spirit would lay waste to white
supremacist Christianity. Ring shouts would conjure this Spirit

1. hooks, *Belonging*, 48.
2. Rawick, *The American Slave*, 84.

along with ancestral African spirits, filling those who dared to join this secret church with a power that could not be chained. The Bible became a talking book where reading ability wasn't necessary to learn the story-songs of the faith, the *true* stories of liberation and freedom, not the coopted Pauline narratives of mastery. Liturgical elements included sodden blankets and an overturned pot, to muffle the sounds of such Christian joy. In these hush harbors, a church was born: a church riskier, and in greater rhythm and reliance with the natural world, than any we've known. With the risk came the reward: an untamed Spirit discovered in the ring shout, where biblical languages of liberation were learned, and deep African memory was cultivated from earth, branch, root, and sky. This Spirit of the hush harbors persists still in our times.

With the decline of the church in North America, Black faith leaders in the twenty-first century are grappling with how to organize in the midst of change. Womanist theologian Dr. Chanequa Walker-Barnes in her article "Why I Gave Up Church" articulates this grappling happening in off-the-grid spiritual communities as she says that these spaces are where:

> People [are] tackl[ing] tough questions about faith (and not just Christianity); where they venerate poetry as canonical expressions of who God is and what God is doing in the world; where the hymnody includes Beyoncé's "Freedom," Kendrick Lamar's "Fear," and Susan Werner's "Why Is Your Heaven So Small;" where they pour libations to the ancestors; where they meditate and walk labyrinths; where they talk self-care and empowerment and learn to love and accept themselves as "fearfully and wonderfully made" in the image of God (Psalm 139:14); and where they support and sustain one another as they engage in the struggle for justice in the world. They are places where people find Jesus. These communities are often small and scattered . . . They often do not call themselves church, but that is precisely what they are. It is my hope that they will become a leavening agent for US Christianity and that one day they will be the normative image of what 'church' is. Or at the very least, perhaps

they will proliferate enough that those of us in . . . exile
can more readily connect with them.[3]

These times are not *only* calling for the church to develop a
new political strategy or for our social justice groups to develop a
new faith-rooted approach. Something more radical, at the roots,
is being called forth. We must rethink what the church is from the
ground up. That the church itself must be a cultural strategy for
political transformation. As the radical social historian Jeff Chang
contends: "Cultural change always precedes political change."[4]

Throughout history it is the work of church planting to spread
Christianity among new people and places. Church planting as a
missionary strategy is how the religious right has spread white
supremacist, hetero-patriarchal capitalism and the toxic Christian
nationalism that upholds it. The Black Church and other social
justice–oriented church traditions—especially those of us who
consider ourselves radical and leftist—must deploy missional innovation as a cultural strategy for political and economic transformation in the US. This calls for an emergent liberative ecclesiology
to be a movement that would organize new disciples not crowds,
commit to base building not platform building, form sacred circles
not elitist hierarchies, embody a radical politics not only seek to
change politics in the public square.

There are diverse faith communities of contemplative activism that center and are led by Black and other historically marginalized persons emerging across the US independent from and
on the edges of religious institutions. These communities gather
in homes, coffee shops, schools, community centers, outdoors,
online, and in the streets. We seek the proliferation and equipping
of these communities, through drawing from the wisdom of the
antebellum hush harbors as a promising model of a church movement that was both liberating of the society and the wider church.
Like the hush harbors, developing a vision of church from the margins is to develop decolonizing monastic missional communities,

3. Walker-Barnes, "Why I Gave Up Church."
4. Chang, *Who We Be*, 6.

faith-rooted small groups on the fringes characterized by radical formation, friendship, and fierce revolution. In these spiritually and politically volatile times, equipping churches from the margins to go viral is critical for us to get free.

The Eight Marks

UBUNTU
A deep mutual care and welcome rooted in our interconnectedness.

While we call ourselves a church, we do church differently, so I would describe it as a community of people who support each other . . . and we bring Jesus' teachings to life in a different way, so that it's not about being saved, it's about us having authentic relationships with each other and living in community.

—member-leader, Good Neighbor Movement

They first ask each other how they feel, the state of their minds . . . The slave forgets all his sufferings, except to remind others of the trials during the past week, exclaiming, "Thank God, I shall not live here always!" Then they pass from one to another, shaking hands, and bidding each other farewell, promising, should they meet no more on earth, to strive and meet in heaven, where all is joy, happiness, and liberty. As they separate, they sing a parting hymn of praise.

—enslaved preacher Peter Randolph, describing the hush harbors[1]

1. Sernett, *African American Religious History*, 67.

Reflection on Ubuntu
VENNEIKIA SAMANTHA WILLIAMS

"A person is a person through other persons," says Archbishop Desmond Tutu.[2] In a traditional reading of the biblical story of Creation, there was just one thing that was not good, and that was for a person to be alone. God fixed this by giving the first human ever created the gift of companionship with another person. When God saw this, it was declared that this was "very good."

"Ubuntu" is a Southern African principle concerning oneness, collectivism, and basic human kindness. The Zulu phrase in which "ubuntu" is found, *umuntu ngumuntu ngabantu*, literally translates to "a person is a person (through other) persons." No one person can meet all their needs and achieve every one of their goals without the help of another. The philosophy of Ubuntu tells us that we are interconnected and can only thrive through interdependency.

Interdependency and collectivism are largely discouraged and dis-incentivized in most American and Western contexts. If individualism continues to be the dominating principle and defining mark of the society and congregations, it will be the death of us and all we hold dear.

The practice of meeting each other's needs amongst and by the people was commonplace in Black community and family life in antebellum times. All that we might have need of was "in the room." It had to be. While we could wait for those with an abundance of power and resources to be benevolent and humane, instead we decided to be the doctor, teacher, preacher, artisan, and whatever else was needed to both survive and thrive.

In the 1960s, The Black Panther Party for Self-Defense taught us about this type of people power. Through the creation of feeding programs, rideshares, ambulance services, and more, they protected and served their neighbors. They countered the efforts

2. Desmond Tutu, quoted in Templeton Prize, "Who We Are: Human Uniqueness and the African Spirit of Ubuntu," YouTube video, 03:26, https://www.youtube.com/watch?v=owZtfqZ271w.

of white, capitalist endeavors to eliminate and disempower them with the services and education their community needed.

The account of the earliest church in Acts 2:44 shows us this type of collectivism that requires getting close to people, building trust, knowing people's names and their stories. These early believers were all together and had all things in common. They knew if their neighbor had a need because they were in proximity and in frequent conversation. From a place of knowing, trusting, and being with one another, they made sure to find tangible solutions to the material conditions their neighbors faced.

Hezekiah Walker's song, "I Need You to Survive" beautifully describes ubuntu:

> I need you, you need me.
> We're all a part of God's body . . .
> It is [God's] will, that every need be supplied.
> You are important to me, I need you to survive.[3]

The biblical principles of being a body of many parts and bearing one another's burdens must be remembered, internalized, and lived out faithfully. This is where our healing lies. This is where our power lies.

As our structures and institutions currently stand, we have a long way to go before things are stable and life-giving, especially our churches. There is more often concern for maintaining a brand than meeting the needs of the people in the congregation, or the neighborhood the church is in. There is more often concern for amassing more numbers of people in pews and on screens than tending to the people in our immediate circle, getting to know them and how our destinies are intertwined. The parish or neighborhood-based model of church has become replaced with commuter church. We must know and believe that our well-being is tied up with the well-being of the people in closest proximity to us, and to all those that are oppressed. Up the street and around the corner. The needs of our neighbors must be taken seriously.

---

3. Walker, "I Need You to Survive."

adrienne maree brown, author of *Emergent Strategy*, helps us further understand ubuntu when she says this about social movements and building people power: "The idea of interdependence is that we can meet each other's needs in a variety of ways, that we can truly lean on others and they can lean on us."[4]

Even the trinitarian relationship between the God Who Parents, the Son, and the Holy Spirit models for us how we ought to love and long for one another. How to make room for one another. Depend on one another. How we might testify to the glory we see in one another. Ubuntu makes interpersonal, political, and theological demands of us:

- a redistribution and equitable sharing of resources;
- a hospitality for the "person passing through";[5] and
- a respect for and celebration of the different skills and ways of making meaning in the world.

If I have and my neighbor does not, they cannot continue to go without for long. This is an opportunity to build intimacy and for reciprocity, with the unspoken commitment that they would do the same for me if and when my time comes. We are only as strong as our most vulnerable neighbor. Our elderly neighbor. Our trans neighbor. Our incarcerated neighbor.

We have been shown and have always known: we all we got. We must not forget one another. Along with our remembrance, we must show up in tangible ways for each other.

Feed one another. Love on our kids. Create and maintain sharing circles. Be for one another what "they" never have and never will be for us.

This is what the hush harbors modeled for us. This is what community should look like.

4. brown, *Emergent Strategy*, 87.

5. Nelson Mandela, quoted in Samuel Bartolo, "The Concept of 'Ubuntu'—Nelson Mandela," YouTube video, 01:36, https://www.youtube.com/watch?v=D2lWQ6XvVgY.

STAY WOKE

Awakening to the rupturing grief that slavery never ended—a sacred attention and care for bodies in captivity and for bodies crying out for hope.

Whatever needs to be done to take care of the people where they are is what we take care of.
—member-leader, New Birth Community AME Church

We're always coming back to the Christian story. That theme of escape, of resistance to empire, that's always coming back.
—Greg Jarrell, QC Family Tree

I know that some day we'll be free and if we die before that time our children will live to see it.
—George Womble, formerly enslaved[6]

Were the slave preachers a force for accommodation to the status quo or a force for the exercise of slave autonomy? On the one hand, the slave preacher was criticized by former slaves as the "mouthpiece of the masters." On the other hand, some slave preachers preached and spoke of freedom in secret.[7]

Reflection on Stay Woke
TERRANCE HAWKINS

I.

In the opening pages of his classic book *Jesus and the Disinherited,* the prophetic mystic and pastoral counselor of the civil rights

6. Raboteau, *Slave Religion,* 156.
7. Raboteau, *Slave Religion,* 156.

movement, Howard Thurman, shared the story of an encounter he had in 1935 while traveling in India. After giving a talk at a college in Ceylon, he was invited by the school's principal to a sit down over coffee. Thurman recounted how the principal pressed him with the following barrage of questions:

"What are you doing over here? This is what I mean.

"More than three hundred years ago your fore[parents] were taken from the western coast of Africa as slaves [sic]. The people who dealt in the slave traffic were Christians. . . . The name of one of the famous British slave vessels was 'Jesus.'

"The men who bought the slaves were Christians. Christian ministers, quoting the Christian apostle Paul, gave the sanction of religion to the system of slavery. . . . During all the period since then you have lived in a Christian nation in which you are segregated, lynched, and burned. Even in the church, I understand, there is segregation. One of my students who went to your country sent me a clipping telling about a Christian church in which the regular Sunday worship was interrupted so that many could join a mob against one of your fellows. When he had been caught and done to death, they came back to resume their worship of their Christian God.

"I am a Hindu. I do not understand. Here you are in my country, standing deep within the Christian faith and tradition. I do not wish to seem rude to you. But, sir, I think you are a traitor to all the darker peoples of the earth. I am wondering what you, an intelligent man, can say in defense of your position."[8]

Thurman's response to these piercing questions is what followed in the pages of *Jesus and the Disinherited*. In it, he performed two very necessary interventions in the dominating framework of white-ameri-christianity. First, he (re)situated Jesus in his first-century social context. It was, as theologian Wil Gafney recently said of her own work, a "redirec[ting] . . . to the sacred texts of the Afro-Asiatic people who inhabited the African tectonic plate of the

8. Thurman, *Jesus and the Disinherited*, 15.

Afro-Syrian rift that opens up in the bed of the Jordan River into the Great Rift Valley of East Africa."[9] For centuries, Jesus had been extracted from his Jewishness, and the revolutionary rabbi from Nazareth's social status as a member of a poor, oppressed, stigmatized minority community had been rendered inconsequential. Yet, Thurman saw this as an essential interpretive key in understanding the Gospel. From this place, Thurman put forth the powerful and largely overlooked truth that the Jesus movement did not begin and end with a call for "the haves to help the have nots." Rather, the movement of God in Christ started at the margins, with the "have nots" at the center of divine activity. Howard argued that Jesus was the divine embodiment of what it looks like for those "who live with their backs against the wall" to practice the kind of freedom of spirit, soul, and body that births new worlds into being.

One could trace the genealogical roots of Thurman's faith to the Africanized and liberatory Christianity practiced by enslaved Black people in the hush harbors of the antebellum south. These secret, illegal worship gatherings, deep in the brush, under the cover of night, were the very antithesis of the sanctioned worship gatherings that took place under the "master's gaze" on the plantation. As their enslavers slept both physically and spiritually, Africans scurried wide awake to the woods and swamps, encountering a healing and liberating Presence in the womb of the night. Contrary to what some would have us believe, these were not mindless, helpless, hoodwinked souls being ushered into the "sunken place" of white supremacy via Christianity. No, these were intelligent, intuitive, spiritually conscious, freedom-pursuing people who found in the story of Jesus, of Moses, of Esther, and of Mary, a God who was in deep solidarity with them. The stories of the Bible may have been "new to their ears," but as the writings of the formerly enslaved Igbo abolitionist Olaudah Equiano reveal, the cosmologies and truths embedded within these stories were in no way foreign to their understanding of the world. There was profound resonance, "deep calling unto deep." Therefore, their embrace of Christ shouldn't be understood as a wholesale shedding of their indigenous spiritualities.

9. Wil Gafney (@WilGafney), Twitter, October 27, 2019, 8:04 a.m., https://twitter.com/wilgafney/status/1188471662716563458?s=21.

It was an ingenious wedding of the two. As royal image-bearers of God, they were, in the words of John the Revelator, "bringing their glory into it." Theologian Eboni Marshall Turman described the phenomenon this way: "We took our gods . . . went into the woods . . . and found Jesus for ourselves."[10]

Before her, Howard Thurman wrote, "By some amazing but vastly creative insight, they undertook the redemption of the religion that the master had profaned in their midst.[11]" They may have been step-children of the empire, "pre-destined" by the religion of whiteness to be a right-less, landless, brutalized people, but in the hush harbor they laid hold of their belovedness as children of a liberating God. A God, who in the words of the negro spiritual, had given them "the right to the tree of life!"

II.

The encounter Thurman had with the Indian principal feels eerily familiar for those of us who remain rooted in the story of the life-acts, death, and resurrection of Jesus of Nazareth in this socio-political moment. We are understandably pressed with questions by Black kinfolk about our embrace of a faith that has been used to deface our people. To varying degrees of intensity, they declare that Black folk have foolishly and sheepishly worshiped our oppressor's God to our own demise. They say that the religion was violently forced upon us via enslavement and we must fervently reject it if we are ever to be free. We must not cower at these critiques, nor dismiss the place that they come from. Especially in this apocalyptic hour when God is allowing folks to pull the covers off of the American mythos of a pure, innocent, Judeo-Christian city shining on a hill. Their suspicion is not baseless! The trauma of "plantation religion" runs through their/our bloodline. It's in their/our bodies. It's bone deep!

Instead, we must lean into the questions, feeling their weight. We must embody the posture of what could be called "a church in

10. Landis-Aina, "Resistance and Ritual from the Margins," para. 1.

11. Thurman, *Deep River and the Negro Spiritual Speaks of Life and Death*, 40.

the wake." Here, I'm riffing off the work of author Christena Sharp. In her book *In the Wake: On Blackness and Being*, she builds on the "metaphor of the wake in the entirety of its meanings.[12]" The wake is "the keeping watch with the dead, the path of a [slave] ship, the consequence of something . . . awakening, and consciousness."[13] Her language of "in the wake" disrupts the unhelpful and even harmful binary of "woke" versus "un-woke." It is much more accurate to say that we are "in the wake." We are on a journey of being awakened. There is no arrogance-inducing pinnacle to reach. It's a never-ending, humbling, life-long process of embodied learning and unlearning.

A "church in the wake" has come to see that we live in the afterlife of slavery. Or said another way, churches in the wake are developing consciousness around the ways in which the US is haunted, hunted, and enslaved by the idolatrous forces that brought into being chattel slavery and Jim Crow. Even though these manifestations have "officially ended," they remain inside of the body politic of this nation. We must come to see anti-Blackness, indigenous dispossession, and the slave/master relationship as an enduring soul-cial virus infecting every square inch of this settler colonialist nation. For this reason, the hush harbor's "fugitive" expression of church remains relevant. It reminds us that to be a disciple of Jesus is to be undisciplined by the unholy and unjust patterns of the world (Rom 12:1–2). The ways of being Black that birthed the subversive psalms we call "spirituals"—concocted healing balms in the midst of plantation-life trauma, incubated revolts, and organized escapes—hold within them generative possibilities for the present.

A "church in the wake" is able to hold in tension the reality that there have always been two dueling forms of Christianity. "Jesus of Norway" versus Jesus of Nazareth—the brown Palestinian Afro-Asiatic Jew who proclaimed the reign of God in the face of Imperial Rome's occupation. The plantation gospel of Jonathan Edwards versus the abolitionist gospel of Frederick Douglass. White Jesus—the cosmic tool of the powerful—versus the lynched—but resurrected "Black Christ" who co-conspires with the powerless. There have always been those who have worshiped the empire as

12. Sharp, *In the Wake*, 17.
13. Sharp, *In the Wake*, 17–18.

if it were god. And there have always been those who have resisted the empire because they knew it wasn't God. Black folks (and their accomplices), rooted in the empire-resisting faith of Jesus, have prayed for a Kin-dom of justice, peace, and joy in the Holy Spirit to come on earth as it is in heaven. There have always been heralds of an alt-Gospel who pray an alt-Lord's prayer:

> Our founding fathers who art in heaven. Hallowed be thy names. Thy empire come, thy will be gun. On this stolen earth as it is in heaven. Give us this day, the daily bread of racism. And forgive us our trespasses as we refuse to forgive those who trespass our borders. Lead us not into paying reparations and deliver us from equality. For thine is the injustice, the idolatry, and inhumanity forever and ever.

Sadly, there are present day and historic examples of oppressed people internalizing this form of Christianity. Some of our own kinfolk are possessed by a "white Jesus." We must perform exorcisms. The "church in the wake" has the prophetic courage and compassion to stand flat-footed, but teary-eyed, saying to them, "who has bewitched you?"

> America is not the Kin-dom of God.
> Jesus is not the constitution made flesh.
> Racial capitalism is not the economy of God.
> The US Military is not God's messianic global police force.
> "The National Anthem is not a Psalm."[14]
> We are not called to preach the sermon of Mount Rushmore.
> "Make America Great Again" is not the church's creed.
> God is not a patron of the American Empire.
> Nationalism is not pure and undefiled religion.
> Whiteness does not equal "Christ-likeness."
> Queer and trans-antagonism is not the Gospel.
> Choose this day whom you will worship and serve.
> Will you be a "cross-bearer or a flag waver?"[15]

14. Quote inspired by Bernice King (@BerniceKing), Twitter, August 14, 2017, 6:52 p.m., https://twitter.com/berniceking/status/897244468348432384?lang=en.

15. Inspired by Cornel West, quoted in Christopher Lydon, "Cornel West on Why James Baldwin Matters More Than Ever," para. 17.

III.

The church in the wake pushes against Western dualism in its pursuit of transformative justice. Like Harriet, Sojourner, and Fannie the church in the wake is unapologetic about its mysticism. Communion with the Spirit precedes, sustains, and propels its activism. The church in the wake knows that the social is spiritual and that the spiritual is social. She understands that human beings are "inspirited bodies and embodied spirits."[16] They know that societies are ordered by inspirited structures and structural manifestations of spiritual realities. The church in the wake embraces the cosmology of the ancestors. This means that awakening to the revolutionary love of God is her chief aim in all things, and that undoing oppression requires both material and immaterial resources.

> The church [in the wake] must be reminded that it is not the master or the servant of the state, but rather the conscience of the state. It must be the guide and the critic of the state, and never its tool. If the church does not recapture its prophetic zeal, it will become an irrelevant social club without moral or spiritual authority.[17]

It was harder to be lulled to sleep as Donald Trump laid bare the imperialist soul of America, making plain and obvious what was hidden to far too many before his ascension. However, the Biden-Harris administration—who is primarily tasked with saving empire and capital—seeks to drowse the restless masses with piecemeal concessions, symbolism, and hollow representation. As the "quintuplet evils" of racism, capitalism/poverty, militarism, heteropatriarchy, and the "plantationocene"[18] (climate change) threaten existence itself, may we dig our heels in as the "church in the wake."

Stay woke!

16. See President's Council on Bioethics, *Being Human*.

17. King, "A Knock at Midnight."

18. Proposed alternate name for the human geological epoch often called the "Anthropocene." See Davis et al., "Anthropocene, Capitalocene, . . . Plantationocene?," for a way of speaking about the ecological crisis or climate change by centering racial justice and the history of plantations in the analysis.

NORTH STAR

Building a new and better world in the midst of the
unjust world that's passing away.

Is it even possible to have church in a way that is liberative given the current container or does the container
just need to be demolished?

—Helms Jarrell, QC Family Tree

Everything is not in the building. Sometimes we've got to
go some places to see the Lord's work. We have to travel
together.

—Leader, New Birth Community AME Church

I don't think healing for us is particularly a destination.
It's always something we're striving towards, on the journey to.

—ministry partner, The Gathering

Enslaved women impersonated white women, disguised
themselves as white male slaveholders, posed as Black
male soldiers, faked physical and mental illnesses, served
as spies, mailed themselves north as cargo, joined others
on the Underground Railroad, boarded ships headed to
Africa, and committed mercy killings in order to protect
their children from slavery. They risked their lives in creative and subversive ways because they believed they had
a right, as one former enslaved man stated, "to own your
own body."[19]

I asked Mama Freeney if she had ever heard of Harriet
Tubman, and she told me, "Yes, I've heard of Harriet
Tubman. Grandma Rye talked about her . . . but there

---

19. Harrison, *Enslaved Women and the Art of Resistance in Antebellum
America*, 180.

were a lot of Harriets. Women like her, you know. And men too."[20]

Reflection on North Star
ANTHONY SMITH

The North Star, also called Polaris, is a star in the constellation Ursa Minor. For centuries this major astronomical body hung from the heavens giving navigational aid to travelers. By sea or land, this North Star was a ready reference gifting explorers and merchants (both ancient and modern) coordinates to worlds known and unknown.

The North Star is the north star because of its usual placement in the sky that led travelers to the northern parts of the globe. In the case of runaway enslaved Africans in the Antebellum South, the North Star would lead them to northern free territories. Enslaved Africans waged many kinds of struggle to set off on their path guided by this star: armed rebellions, disguise, the Underground Railroad, purchasing their freedom, burning slaveholder property, and more. Following this large celestial body in the night sky would lead them to new worlds. Many of our ancestors would follow this star all the way to Canada. It is in these northern places, away from the surveillance of slavocracy, that they would build new lives and worlds for their children and descendants.

The North Star, for participants in hush harbors, came to symbolize the possibility of a new world. A free and just world. A world free of domination and oppression. For those that participate in modern day hush harbors or Liberating Churches, the North Star may not be a faraway geographical location. The North Star may be a reference point to the new world the Spirit is making in our midst. The North Star may be more than a pointer to a new spot on the planet for us to sojourn to (it can still be that too). For those of us on the collective journey of decolonizing our souls, the North Star points to new theological and ecclesiological coordinates *locii imperium* (in the heart of empire).

20. Harding and Freeney, *Remnants*, 12.

The North Star represents what Canadian philosopher Charles Taylor calls a "social imaginary, a broad understanding of the way a given people imagine their collective social life."[21] We see this idea exemplified in the baptismal story of Jesus as told in the gospel of Mark. When Jesus comes out of the baptismal waters of the Jordan he is possessed by the Holy Spirit. As we follow the sequence, we see the Spirit, like a dove, tear open the old world. The dove, representing a new world, harkening back to the story of Noah and the Ark alerts everyone that a new world has arrived.[22] The Spirit's landing and possession of Jesus is also the landing and possession of the possibility of a new world. Jesus is anointed with Heavenly Spirit power to build a new world. For those of us that participate in Liberating Churches, we should see that to be filled with the Spirit is to be filled with the grace and energy to struggle and build a new world in the midst of the old one characterized by idolatry and oppression.

The North Star represents the Spirit's desire and prefigurative presencing of free zones in the midst of the Global Capital Order.[23] It is the new social imaginary that unleashes the possibility of a new way of being in the world. North Star spaces gift us coordinates to liberation in the midst of shrinking publics, commons, and spaces needed to cultivate our imaginations and attune our bodies to the Spirit of liberation already at work in our communities. This is beyond relevant in the age and specter of neoliberalism, a worldview, a political and economic frame that has storied all aspects of our culture: austerity measures, privatization, hyper-individualism, diminishing social democracy. The neoliberal revolution was captured succinctly by former British Prime Minister Margaret Thatcher in the 1980s: "There is no such thing as society. There are only individuals and families." The specter of neoliberalism meant to safeguard free-market capitalism and individual liberty set in motion a cultural torrent that diminished and incapacitated

21. Taylor, *Modern Social Imaginaries*, back cover.

22. Myers, *Binding the Strong Man*.

23. *Prefigurative politics* are the modes of organization and social relationships that strive to reflect the future society being sought by the group.

public goods (institutionalized ways American society sought aid and justice for the poor). The cultural implications of this attack upon the common good and sense of collective responsibility has created a deep hunger and desire for community and shared sense of social justice. North Star communities can be an antibody to this pervasive decommunitization of human connection.

Building a North Star community is an ongoing journey of learning, unlearning, and relearning. It requires practicing radical hospitality by being a vital part of the organic community organizing and activism in your city. Building toward the North Star means practicing radical hospitality by opening our spaces to all concerned community members. It is to celebrate the arts, practice storytelling, speak to justice issues, and ultimately to build community together in a sea of loneliness. These are just small contributions to the larger work of creating new maps with ancient coordinates that lead to liberation and love.

ALL GOD'S CHILDREN GOT SHOES

Equitable leadership and accessible preaching that affirms everyone's gifts and abilities to be leader-full.

> . . . we had tag team preaching by people who are not ordained, by people who don't have a masters of divinity because the word is in everyone. The delivery may be different, but everybody has a word so it reinforces our sense of equality.
>
> —member-leader, New Birth Community AME Church

> [We are not looking for] sheep and that's what's really important to me . . . I'm responsible for coming, bringing something to the meeting, giving and receiving, taking the initiative for my own spiritual development . . . So it's more about building a life and building lives together

than just coming to a place to read and learn about God or Jesus, it's more about bringing Jesus to life in ourselves and each other.

—member-leader, Good Neighbor Movement

We don't use the words "members." We use "missioners." A member is someone that comes and more or less is put in their place and receives orders. Missioners, they come to give back and be sent out.

—George, Mission House

The old folks used to slip out in the fields and thickets to have prayer meetings and my mother always took me along for fear something would happen to me if left behind. They would all get around a kettle on their hands and knees and sing and pray and shout and cry. My mother was a great prayer and shouter and she always asked God to take care of her son—meaning me.

—formerly enslaved man[24]

Everyone was so anxious to have a word to say that a preacher did not have a chance. All of them would sing and pray.

—Hanna Lowery, a formerly enslaved African[25]

[AME Bishop Alexander] Payne, during his visits to brush arbor meetings throughout the American colonies, was outraged by Blacks' participation in ring shouts. Payne viewed ring shouting as "heathenish" practices, a "disgrace" to the "Black race" and the "Christian name . . ." Payne ordered the pastors and participants to stop dancing and in most cases the congregation complied. Two women at the Bethel Church in Baltimore, Maryland, however, galvanized the congregation and fought back. Ring shouting was their "primary means of contact with and respect for ancestral spirits and the source of artistic expression" and spiritual renewal; many enslaved and free Africans believed there could be "no Christian conversion except through the ring." The two women

24. Rawick, *The American Slave*, 147–48.
25. Rawick, *The American Slave*, 76.

rejected Payne's demands and "rose from a front row and approached the pulpit with clubs, and attacked Payne and an assistant pastor."[26]

Reflection on All God's Children Got Shoes
LAURA BYRCH

I got shoes,
you got shoes,
all God's children got shoes.
When I get to heaven gonna put on my shoes,
gonna walk all over God's heaven, heaven,
gonna walk all over God's heaven.
Everybody talking about heaven ain't goin' there,
heaven, heaven.[27]

In the few short lines of this well-known spiritual, enslaved Africans in pre-Civil War America proclaimed radical truths about themselves and their understanding of God as a God of justice. First, they affirmed that they were God's children, who would one day be with God in heaven. Second, that God would meet every need and judge the hearts of all, showing a reversal of the slaveholding society's notions of who true Christians were and were not.

Those who sang this song took to heart the stories of Genesis 1–2: that humankind is made in the image of God and tasked with wisely leading the world. Human beings are entrusted with the responsibility to help shape the world according to God's will. Slaveholders who called themselves Christians were greatly abusing this authority and perverting notions of what was God's will, but through this song, enslaved Africans claimed authority to narrate what God's will truly was and is.

Writing about this spiritual, Howard Thurman said:

26. Harrison, *Enslaved Women and the Art of Resistance in Antebellum America*, 211–12.

27. Jackson, "Walk Over God's Heaven."

25

This is one of the authentic songs of protest. It was sung in anticipation of a time that even yet has not fully come—a time when there shall be no slave row in the church, no gallery set aside for the slave, no special place, no segregation, no badge of racial and social stigma, but complete freedom of movement. Even at that far-off moment in the past, these early singers put their fingers on the most vulnerable spot in Christianity and democracy. The wide, free range of his spirit sent him in his song beyond all barriers. In God's presence at least there would be freedom; slavery is no part of the purpose or the plan of God.[28]

Despite the harsh realities of slavery, where plantation Christianity was twisted and weaponized by white masters to try to keep enslaved Black people subordinate and submissive, Black communities of enslaved peoples still encountered the God of justice, who revealed to them a message of dignity, equality, and belovedness that they put to song. It was a message that affirmed that those who were suffering under slavery were God's children, made in God's image, and that one day not only would their needs be met, but there would be freedom to roam all over heaven. No more passes or papers needed, in fact, the preachers and adherents of slaveholder religion—with their talk of heaven and lack of Christlike behavior—would not even make it to heaven.

Holding in their hearts and minds this vision of the boundaryless freedom that awaited them in heaven, individuals who were enslaved found courage to run away to earthly freedom in the North.

As a white person, my earliest memory of this song is of singing it in children's choir at church. Looking back, our "Cherub Choir," made up of little white smiling faces and tiny feet wearing patent leather shoes, really had no business singing this song. We couldn't really imagine what it would be like to not have shoes, much less to not be allowed to have shoes. We had closets full of shoes, and as we grew up, we would encounter few barriers to freedom to go and do as we pleased. Sure, our choir director and

28. Thurman, *Deep River*, 48.

parents tried to explain that this song was about God wanting everyone to have what they need. But I don't remember any mention of why the song was created or the dynamics between white slaveholders and enslaved Africans that led to a people singing about shoes and freedom in heaven. We certainly left out the part about "everybody talking about heaven ain't goin' there." No one wanted to talk about how our freedom and dignity was still something society guaranteed for people who looked like us or how the world we would grow up in was still built on denying freedom and full humanity to Black people and people of color.

Learning that song as a child perhaps began to shape in me a vision that my cultural ancestors could not see—the truth that every human being, and especially the enslaved people who created the song—were made in the image of God, had inherent worth and dignity and deserved basic things like shoes and freedom . . . not only in heaven, but in the here and now. Yet it is not enough for those of us who are the descendants of slaveholder religion to look back and say "yes, everybody should've been given shoes and freedom, equality and dignity back then." We who are white Christians must continue to recognize and dismantle the ways our religious beliefs and practices, our economic policies, and the laws and norms our people have created are steeped in the white supremacy that denies dignity, freedom, and a quality of life to Black people and people of color still today. In light of police brutality and other acts of violence, not seeing the dignity and worth of Black and Brown siblings continues to be a matter of life and death that has left too many dead in the streets. And we must recognize that continuing to live as uncritical heirs to slaveholder religion and the legacy of white supremacy harms us white people too. I believe this is what enslaved Africans meant when they were saying to me and my ancestors that though we talked an awful lot about heaven, we weren't going to see heaven. That we can never fully embrace the beloved community the song points to because we have uncritically internalized white superiority. To the extent that we continue to operate in this way we are not residents and workers of heaven, of beloved community, we actually work against heaven, and especially work against bringing more heaven to earth.

Saying "All God's Children Got Shoes" is a way of claiming dignity that isn't acknowledged in dominant culture. Hush harbors today, as during the time of slavery, continue to proclaim this message and push against dominant society's structural hierarchies of leadership. Even though white men didn't give Black preachers authority to proclaim the Word as it was revealed to them in the antebellum South, Black preachers and believers knew "they had shoes." They learned the stories of Scripture and knew God was not who the slaveholder preachers were trying to convince them God was. They had to trust their own voices, their own interpretation, even as white slaveholders sought to shame and silence them. In hush harbors, they were empowered to freely interpret and preach the Word without authority from any institution or governing body. God gave each enslaved Black person the dignity and ability to understand and proclaim God's truth. Men, women, and even children were seen as leaders and valued members with important contributions to make.

Our churches and communities can begin to live into the mark "All God's Children Got Shoes" when we:

- Practice shared leadership, honoring the gifts each person brings and their unique part in wisely leading us toward the vision of beloved community.

- Center the voices of people and communities that dominant white supremacist patriarchal culture has tried to ignore or silence.

- Create alternative leadership structures that are equitable, consensus-based and characterized by permission-giving instead of the authority to restrict and control being given to a few.

STEAL AWAY

An orientation towards fugitivity to provide an alternative to empire.

They may not come on Sunday, but they join in on mission with us in different ways.

—Anthony Smith, Mission House

So when we first started [as a community] we prayed and we wrote down our list of names of people that we felt compelled to send out an initial invite. And some of those folks didn't respond and we just felt like those who had an ear to hear this weird invitation would jump in. And, those that didn't, you know, weren't to be a part of this move. And then what began to happen, people that were part of the group would run their mouths. They couldn't contain it. It was almost like Jesus telling people "yo don't tell about it." . . . So sometimes people get linked up through finding out from a person that's been a part. And the other piece is this, if you live in this neighborhood or in east Winston or in any way, shape or form you're fighting for Black freedom, you have an open invite, standing invite at all times to engage in the gatherings.

—Terrance Hawkins, Greenway Community

I see individuals who I know are members of other churches, who may not themselves be willing to join a church like ours, but the work we're doing is also meeting a need . . . there is a hunger for this kind of justice work that is happening and it is not being met in those congregations. So people are kind of watching the work that we're doing and the way that, at least, to the extent that they can see it as an outsider, the way that we're structuring our life as a church and are kind of finding hope and inspiration from that.

—Reggie Weaver, Good Neighbor Movement

When de slave go round singin' "Steal Away to Jesus," dat mean dere gwine be a 'ligious meetin' dat night. Dat de sig'fication of a meetin'. De masters 'fore and after freedom didn't like dem 'ligious meetin's, so us natcherly slips off at night, down in de bottoms or somewheres. Sometimes us sing and pray all night.[29]

—a formerly enslaved African

My master used to ask us children, "Do your folks pray at night?" We said, "No," cause our folks had told us what to say. But the Lord have mercy, there was plenty of that going on. They'd pray, "Lord, deliver us from bondage."

—a formerly enslaved African[30]

"We were told that the beating of the drums had a special significance, but that was all we could learn on the subject; we were told that this was a secret, divulged only to members" . . . She [ex-slave interviewee] remembered hearing the drums beaten to tell the people in the nearby settlements of an approaching dance or festival.

—an interview with a formerly enslaved African[31]

Reflection on Steal Away
BRANDON WRENCHER

In pre-Civil War America, time was indeed a luxury . . . and white folks owned it. Not only were enslaved bodies the property of white slaveholders, there was no place in the plantation economy that was not under the gaze of white patriarchy. Black folks' time was expected to be fully in service to white desires. The law justified it: it was illegal for black folks to congregate. Black folks were constantly under the surveillance of white folks, including being

29. Harrison, *Enslaved Women and the Art of Resistance in Antebellum America*, 203.

30. Callahan, *The Talking Book*, 88.

31. Harrison, *Enslaved Women and the Art of Resistance in Antebellum America*, 198.

watched by the black folks that white folks controlled. Breaking
this law meant being whipped, and at worst death. When they sang
"steal away, steal away to Jesus . . . I ain't got long to stay here"[32] in
the plantation fields, enslaved Africans were signaling in code that
freedom would never be given to them. The untrained ear thought
they were talking about the afterlife. The trained ear knew they
meant they'd have to steal away freedom, to take it in the here and
now if it were ever to come. Stealing away became a metaphor for a
lifestyle of fugitivity and holy deception. The bending and twisting
of lyrics and branches gave cues to the path through the woods of
one of the most significant sites of freedom, the hush harbor.

> From the abundant testimony of fugitive and freed slaves
> it is clear that the slave community had an extensive reli-
> gious life of its own, hidden from the eyes of the master.
> In the . . . seclusion of the brush arbors ("hush harbors")
> the slaves made a Christianity truly their own.[33]

There were regular opportunities for enslaved Africans to
worship on the plantation—in racially integrated churches led by
white folks. They could also attend segregated worship gatherings
led by black preachers. Even black worship on the plantation was
supervised by a white minister and assimilated to white religious
structures and customs. Plantation church was shallow, operating
by a religious and racial symbolism, a performative Christianity
and blackness that accommodated racial capitalism and kept the
chattel slavery system uninterrupted. Yet a remnant of enslaved
Africans chose to steal away to worship in the hush harbor, dissat-
isfied with white and black plantation churches. The appeal of the
hush harbors was both liturgical and political. Like the liberation
they sought from the plantation economy, the hush harbor was a
site to liberate Christianity in service to the well-being and freedom dreams of enslaved Africans. This meant participation in the
hush harbor was by invitation. Enslaved Africans were vetted and
vouched for to demonstrate political solidarity to enter the hush

32. Boatwright, "Steal Away."
33. Raboteau, *Slave Religion*, 212.

harbors. The integrity and safety of the hush harbor depended on a vow of its members to betray the plantation religion and economy. To steal away was an act of putting their lives and bodies on the line. One formerly enslaved African says this about the quality of the commitment of a member of the hush harbor, preferring it to the open weekly worship in buildings made accessible after emancipation:

> Meetings back there meant more than they do now. Then everybody's heart was in tune, and when they called on God they made heaven ring. It was more than just a Sunday meeting and then no godliness for a week. They would steal off to the fields and in the thickets and there ... they called on God out of heavy hearts.[34]

The practice of stealing away put enslaved Africans squarely within the tradition of Jesus. Jesus engaged in holy deception by speaking in parables, riddles, and questions to confound the comfortable and comfort the castaway. Jesus engaged in fugitivity by breaking the laws and customs of the religious and social establishment in service to the poor, the imprisoned, the stranger, the unclean, the sick. Jesus vetted the crowds to invite comrades into an underground circle of revolutionary friendship to transform the society from the inside out.

There are no longer laws that forbid Black people from congregating together, or from worshipping in the manner we choose. Black people are no longer forced to hide our ways of being from the wider society. America and the institutional church would have Black people believe that we can be Black in plain sight. And yet visibility is fool's gold. To be seen is not freedom, not when under the gaze of empire and its chaplains. My ancestors were not forced to steal away. They chose to break rank with the visibility of the plantation culture. They chose risk that brings change. And real change is never about spectacle.

The spectacle of church stood in the way of me truly living into my call as a pastor. Visibility is climbing the clergy corporate

34. Raboteau. *Slave Religion*, 217.

ladder. Saying and doing everything that makes a pastor worthy for the bigger church, bigger salary, bigger brand. Once you reach a certain status then you can say and do what you really believe, not only what would make you likeable. This is the social contract, the grand bribe of the church industrial complex. But I could not fully take the bribe. I could not unhear the closeted stories of queer churchgoers. I could not unsee church members' disgust and discomfort when they were serving houseless neighbors. I could not unfeel the despair in the pit of my stomach from being asked to not preach about and against police brutality. It wasn't long before I reached a breaking point. Not unlike these words from James Baldwin describing his own version of stealing away from plantation religion: "when I faced a congregation, it began to take all the strength I had not to stammer, not to curse, not to tell them to throw away their Bibles and get off their knees and go home and organize, for example, a rent strike."[35]

It took my neighbor, a secular community organizer, to agitate me to steal away. I was complaining about all that I believed was not right with church, and telling him I felt I didn't know what to do. My neighbor said: "That's bullshit, that's internalized oppression. You can learn what to do. If you don't commit to doing things differently, nothing will change."

There were no cameras, no fanfare, no spectacle. This wasn't tweetable. This encounter flies in the face of social media activism and showtime religion. We faced each other. My neighbor practiced the rigor of persuasion and agitation. He challenged me to do something brave. I no longer serve in places I cannot tell the truth and be authentic. I experienced transformation. It hurt like hell. Because hell is what needed to come out of me, all of the conditioning that tells us that everything that glitters is gold and that some expert is going to save us. To steal away is to practice a different conditioning, of regularly challenging each other, as everyday radical disciples, in small, discreet, and direct ways, to break free from the assimilating patterns that prop up our own and others' oppression. No mics, no stages, no shortcuts. Some might call it

35. Baldwin, *The Price of the Ticket*, 353.

old-fashioned discipleship, or organizing conversations. We must normalize these conversations, of stealing away to meet on porches, at bars, in parks, on the block, at the corner store, on hikes, at dinner, in the garden. Everyday people who make sanctuaries of the ordinary, the profane, the small. In these encounters we can be brave with each other. Conversations between those of us already in the movement, to help each other develop and deepen our skills and commitment. And meeting with neighbors who have not already committed their lives to liberation. To help them see their own power. To bring them into the movement, one conversation, one small group at a time. This is stealing away, falling in love over and over again with making dissident disciples of the justice and love revolution.

SANKOFA

Wisdom that is rooted in memory, place, and embodiment of the ancestral Spirit.

Well I think in our preaching, for me personally, you know, I'll talk about ancestors a lot. I also love it that often in our preaching I've even heard prayers talking about the ancestors. I like to believe we reach and get the teachings of our ancestors and that's the things that we try to teach to honor them.

—Dr. Irie Session, The Gathering

We make sure we fill those Bible studies with quotes from scripture, but also quotes from Black ancestors and Brown ancestors. So, you know, obviously, Martin and Harriet and a lot of Fannie Lou Hamer, Ella Baker, and then James Baldwin, and Audre Lorde. Those folks are always like our interlocutors.

—Terrance Hawkins, Greenway Community

To be able to have a spiritual community that is multicultural, to know that we can do things that are not so "Christian-like" . . . like lighting candles, setting intentions at an altar, talking to our ancestors, that it's encouraged. That just pushes me forward in how important these hush harbors are in our liberation as we try to find the interconnection between Christianity and our ancestry . . . and also very open to having people from different walks of life.

—member-leader, Good Neighbor Movement

Us ole heads use ter make 'em on de spurn of de moment, after we wrestle wid de Spirit and come thoo. But the tunes was brung from Africa by our grandaddies. Dey was jis 'miliar song . . . dey call em spirituals, case de Holy Spirit done revealed 'em to 'em.

—formerly enslaved woman from Kentucky[36]

Both before and after Emancipation, there were Blacks who held greater confidence in conjurers than in Christian holy men. Griffin Whittier, a former South Carolina slave, recalled how the adults among the more than sixty slaves on his master's plantation would meet secretly on Saturday nights for a 'lil . . . "fun frum de white folks hearin" . . . They felt especially confident because a "Conjun Doc" told them he had put a spell on 'ole Marse so dat he will "blevin ev'y think dat us tole him bout Sa'day night and Sunday morning."[37]

Reflection on Sankofa
JASOLYN HARRIS

Imagine seeing a beautiful bird flying forward, while looking backward. Literally pause for a moment, close your eyes, and attempt to visualize this. You are shocked, maybe even perplexed seeing this mystical creature flying bizarrely, and yet you see something else

36. Raboteau, *Slave Religion*, 116.
37. Jones, *Born a Child of Freedom, Yet a Slave*, 140.

peculiar going on. Not only is this mysterious bird flying forward while looking backward, but it is also carrying a precious egg in its mouth that symbolizes the future. This beautiful, mystical, mysterious bird is called "Sankofa" and it is one of the many Adinkra symbols of the Akan people of West Africa. Sankofa is expressed in the Akan language as *se wo were fi na wasan kofa a yenki* which is translated to mean, "it is not taboo to go back and fetch what is at risk of being left behind." In other words, looking back while simultaneously flying towards our future is not unthinkable, yet necessary so we can go back and get what is in danger of being left in our past.

I grew up in the Black Missionary Baptist Church tradition, shaped by the institution and beliefs of white Western Christianity that strongly encouraged all of us to forget what is behind us and strain toward what is ahead. We were taught to forgive and forget, especially any trauma inflicted upon us from someone in our household family or church family. In my studies at divinity school and experiences with various colleagues of different Christian traditions, I learned that the Black Missionary Baptist Church wasn't the only denomination being taught flawed belief systems. Many Christian church traditions all over the world have been formed by white Western Christian beliefs that contradict the essence and symbol of the Sankofa. Westernized Christianity tells us in more ways than one that it is taboo to go back into our past and there is great risk in looking back into what we left behind.

This is precisely why the Hush Harbors are essential to the journey of a Liberating Church. Black enslaved persons would not and could not forget their lived realities, which were both various rich African traditions and the immense problem of slavery. Among those traditions were the spirituality of the drum to summon the ancestors for support and the power to conjure the natural world with spells and personal artifacts to bring healing to the community or to cause misfortune for slaveholders. Black enslaved persons' lives were at risk if they were to show the fullness of who they were and the richness of their traditions so they had to carve out space where they could remember what they were forced to leave behind. So they would risk their lives on those days they would travel deep into the forest and worship together unapologetically. It was a place and space they could check in with one another, combine their spiritual practices and somehow, someway make it through one more day of an impossible reality. Black enslaved persons refused to forget and somehow envisioned us in the future possibilities.

Unfortunately, the Christian church today as a whole does not serve as a liberating space for many people, people on the margins of society, and particularly not for queer and trans people of color. Historically and currently, the Christian church tradition nearly worldwide has adopted problematic ways of interpreting the Bible (rooted in a Westernized Christian perspective), which has literally convinced many parents, siblings, extended family, friends, and church communities to abandon, leave behind, and forget a vital group of people necessary for the future of the church. The Sankofa can certainly serve as a symbol to remind the church that our collective liberation can be found through an exploration of what our future might hold when we go back and get what we forgot about our past.

The reality is, particularly for many Black people and more specifically Black Christians, we are unaware of our past ancestry, specifically as it relates to Black Queer people and the role we played spiritually in our communities. This adds a more complex layer to the context of the Sankofa symbol and its relation to Liberating Church. How can one remember, and/or go back and get something they didn't know they left behind? For example, in the Dagaaba tribe of the modern region of Burkina Faso, they see LGBTQIAA+[38] people as "having the ability to intercede between the people . . . as a type of gatekeeper who has direct contact with the Divine."[39] As a Black queer femme Pastor, I discovered this vital ancestral knowledge after I graduated with my Master in Divinity from Duke University. What a beautiful piece of information to go

38. LGBTQIAA: Lesbian, Gay, Bisexual, Transgender, Questioning, Intersex, Asexual and Ally

39. Prower, *Queer Magic*.

back and get from the past while simultaneously flying towards the future in the thick of the present day as a church liberator!

As we continue to reflect on the symbol of the Sankofa in relation to the Hush Harbors, Liberating Church, especially for queer and trans people of color, it is vital for the church to continue contemplating not only what it means to be in a continual cycle of transformation but also how we can begin to transfigure. When Jesus took James, Peter, and John to the top of a mountain to pray, Jesus revealed to them Jesus' self as "a complete change or form or appearance into a more beautiful or spiritual state."[40] Jesus transfigured Jesus' self quite possibly to show James, Peter and John a more beautiful future while simultaneously allowing them to see an important part of the past (Elijah's and Moses' presence) and a present reality that was difficult to fully take in (Jesus' most beautiful state, which they never speak of to anyone). Liberating churches through the collective memory and tangible actions of the Hush Harbors in connection to the symbol of the Sankofa helps us to see particularly queer and trans people of color as the link towards a future that remembers to go back and get what we forgot.

JOY UNSPEAKABLE

A Spirit-driven overcoming marked by joy.

You don't know who's going to offer the word that day. You don't know who's going to pray. You don't know if the Holy Spirit comes in.

—member-leader, New Birth Community AME Church

But when you come in here you are likely to get prophesied over, experience the Holy Spirit, you'll see people speaking in tongues. So there's this interesting

40. McKean, *The New Oxford American Dictionary*, s.v. "transfiguration."

relationship between life in the Spirit and the work of
liberation. For me, they're one and the same.

—Anthony Smith, Mission House

Sometime a group of slaves would leave the house and go
on the branches to talk and have pleasure among themselves and when they got ready for such meetings they
would turn a pot down to keep the sound from going in
the direction of their master's house.

—Florence Bailey, formerly enslaved African[41]

De folks 'ud git in er ring an' march 'roun in time ter der
singin' and den w'en dey git wa'amed up, dey shout an'
clap an' dance an' sing. Some on 'em 'ud get weak an' drop
down den de odders 'ud keep on wid de singin' till mos'
come day. Some on de w'ite folkses 'ud whip dar sarbants
effen dey cotch dem at er ring shout meetin.' Buy dey
shore had er big time down in de thickets an' in de deep
woods.

—Lou Austin, formerly enslaved African[42]

Reflection on Joy Unspeakable
HELMS JARRELL

... joy unspeakable is that moment of mystical encounter
when God tiptoes into the hush arbor,
testifies about Divine suffering,
and whispers in our ears,
"Don't forget, I taught you how to fly
on a wing and a prayer,
when you're ready
let's go!"[43]

One Sunday morning, I am attending a church just a few miles
from my neighborhood. Even though close in proximity, it could
not be further away from the people with whom I live and serve.

41. Cade, "Out of the Mouths of Ex-Slaves," 330.

42. Rawick, The American Slave, 150.

43. Holmes, Joy Unspeakable, xvii–xviii.

In this church, you can see visible signs of systemic investment and economic gain. The drive to the church takes me from barbed wire enclosed brownfields, a cement factory, and giant power lines to lush landscaping, stately houses, and underground fiber optics. Unspoken signals of generational affluence and strategic advancement adorn bodies, architecture, and parking lots. Congregants step out of their Teslas wearing bow ties and art necklaces to enter a grand hall adorned with large oil paintings of five white men who served as pastors of this church.

I am here because my husband, a musician, has arranged to play a jazz worship service. The service begins and the singer, Dawn, wakes us from slumber with an energetic "Woke up this morning with my mind stayed on freedom."[44] During the moments of confession, Dawn and the band lead us through "Down by the Riverside." The air is coming alive with rhythm and drums. Our spirits are becoming alive as we join the chorus.

Next, Dawn begins to sing, "Give me a bottle of justice. I'll take that bottle of justice. I hear it'll set you free." Her voice almost growls with conviction. It is as if we can hear not only the voice of Dawn, but also the voice of her ancestors. I am reminded of what I have read about the Hush Harbors, the ecstatic and transcended experience of God permeating the fullness of the cosmos—voice, breath, branches, earth, body, past, and future all exist in this moment.

> For Africans in bondage in the Americas,
> joy unspeakable is that moment of mystical encounter
> when God tiptoes into the hush arbor,
> testifies about Divine suffering,
> and whispers in our ears,
> "Don't forget, I taught you how to fly
> on a wing and a prayer,
> when you're ready
> let's go!"[45]

---

44. Sweet Honey In The Rock, "Woke Up This Morning with My Mind Stayed on Freedom."

45. Holmes, *Joy Unspeakable*, xvii–xviii.

Dawn's body moves in shapes and rhythm that match the message of the song. She places a hand on her heart, reaches up, and grasps for the bottle of justice she is singing about. Her movements are a physical proclamation. The way she moves reminds me of the Hush Harbor practice called the Ring Shout, a ritual practiced by enslaved Africans in the West Indies and the United States. During the Ring Shout, worshippers would move in a circle, their feet and hands in rhythm and concert with one another and with the Spirit. In the Ring Shout, time would slip away as the participants united their breath, minds, and bodies with one another, with God, and with their ancestors. Every moment, movement, and shout, communicating with God.

The song, "Justice" by Cassandra Wilson, begins to capture me. I want for Dawn what she is asking for herself. Yes, God, give Dawn "a slice of opportunity. I hear it'll fill you up!"[46] She reaches out to the congregation, hands open to receive opportunity. Dawn is my friend. I want what Dawn wants. Rejoice with those who rejoice; weep with those who weep (Rom 12:15).

Then the next line in the song hits me hard. "Give me that box of reparations. I'll have that box of reparations. No, not the little one, I want the big one that matches my scars. I think I'll have some of that." My reaction was uncontrollable. Filled with passion, sitting in this affluent church, among silent and upright congregants, I gasped and screamed aloud, "Yes!" I moved to the music, clapped my hands, and begged God, "Please God, give Dawn justice. Give my neighbors justice. Give us Justice."

> Joy Unspeakable
> is not silent.
> it moans, hums, and bends
> to the dancing universe.
> It is a fractal of transcendent hope,
> a hologram of God's heart,
> a black hole of unknowing.[47]

---

46. Wilson, "Justice."
47. Holmes, *Joy Unspeakable*, xvii–xviii.

Dawn's voice is speaking for the oppressed of our society: Black and Brown people, poor people, LGBTQ people, marginalized people. "Give me reparations," she proclaims. Her message clashes with beliefs deeply held in this congregation's culture about its ambitions and worthiness, its sense of propriety and safety. Even so, she is saying them. She's not just saying them, she's singing them, breathing them, embodying them. Rhythm, voice, singing and breathing, calling forth, drawing us toward justice and repair. And it is astounding, marvelous, mysterious. It is miraculous.

A Black woman in this southern, segregated, white, wealthy church embodies a message of joy and justice that strikes the ears, pierces the heart, and woos the soul. How can she have such faith? How is it that her belief is so deep, so strong, so passionate that she can pray for, sing for, hope for anything, much less reparation and wholeness? Within her is an unrelenting assurance of God's abundant reign.

Red-faced and overcome—with embarrassment, thrill, hope, lament, pleading, fear, and trembling—I was experiencing Joy Unspeakable. My attention to what the congregants were feeling became overwhelmed with what I can only describe as the Spirit. After a few moments, though, I looked around to see if anyone else heard what I did. As a white woman, I know well the fear that sets into a room at the word "reparation." I wondered how the other gatherers were feeling. I looked to see if the women were clutching their purses or if the men were reaching for their wallets.

Even in this place, the power of God's Spirit is so fierce in this moment. It makes me want to break my silence and speak bold words of truth—reparation, justice, opportunity, equity—and not just speak the words. Practicing reparation comes at a cost for me. The cost is privilege, whiteness, and comfort. Even so, God's Spirit compels me to want reparation and to work for it. Reparation in this church building might mean dismantling every frame and unearthing every paving stone. It would mean redistribution of wealth and handing over the keys. Though it might mean conflict and sacrifice, with God's Spirit, I am ready for it.

Joy Unspeakable
is both FIRE AND CLOUD,
the unlikely merger of
trance and high tech lives
ecstatic songs and jazz repertoire.
Joy Unspeakable is
a symphony of incongruities
of faces aglow and hearts on fire
and the wonder of surviving together.

At this moment of unspeakable joy, I am reminded of another radical woman of color who sang of great joy in the midst of great sorrow. She prophetically spoke truth to power—casting down the mighty and lifting up the lowly:

My soul magnifies the Lord, and my spirit rejoices in God my Savior, for he has looked with favor on the lowliness of his servant. Surely, from now on all generations will call me blessed; for the Mighty One has done great things for me, and holy is his name. His mercy is for those who fear him from generation to generation. He has shown strength with his arm; he has scattered the proud in the thoughts of their hearts. He has brought down the powerful from their thrones, and lifted up the lowly; he has filled the hungry with good things, and sent the rich away empty. He has helped his servant Israel, in remembrance of his mercy, according to the promise he made to our ancestors, to Abraham and to his descendants forever."

—The Magnificat (Luke 1:46–55 NASB)

In her book, *Joy Unspeakable: Contemplative Practices of the Black Church*, Barbara A. Holmes writes: "There is no response, other than radical love, that is up to the task of healing transgenerational wounds. The healing begins within. Questions that we lay on those inner altars and that receive no response in one generation are handed down to the next."[48]

When you know that this world is not your home because you are deemed to be inferior by virtue of your color, gender,

48. Holmes, *Joy Unspeakable*, 58.

sexual identity, or class status, you must look beyond what can be perceived by the natural eye to find solace. Moses Berry describes this lived transcendence as "always looking beyond the blue." The blue sky was not a roof over their oppression; rather, it was a permeable point of reference for prayer and entreaties.

Joy Unspeakable envisions and embodies all that God is able to do, which is immeasurably more than all we could ask or imagine. It draws us in and entices us to make things right, to tear down walls built to keep people out and status created to keep people down. Joy Unspeakable turns our eyes beyond the blue, to a place where repair is made and justice is sought. It dares us to play and pray. It causes us to practice freedom and sing deliverance even in captivity. And it draws us into community, no longer an architectural structure or artificial construct, but an organic system of memory and responsibility. A people and place of liberation and great unspeakable joy.

TALKING BOOK

Interpreting the Bible as a book that leads to freedom through always searching for Jesus, the Exodus, and Spirit in every passage.

I will speak to the fact that it is not even just within the physical presence of who is in leadership, but in our curriculum building and reading of the Bible we center the work of people of color and queer folks and marginalized folks.

—Kelly Florence, Good Neighbor Movement

Jesus was a foot soldier going into the community healing, staying with people, listening to their stories. That's what we are supposed to be doing. If we're reading Scripture we should be doing what Jesus was doing. People say

you can't be an advocate for the poor and preach. Then,
what Scripture are you reading?

—Toni Smith, Mission House

At least three or four times a year [the master's minis-
ter] used as a text: "Slaves, be obedient to them that are
your masters . . . as unto Christ." Then he would go on to
show how it was God's will that we were slaves and how,
if we were good and happy slaves, God would bless us.
I promised my Maker that if I ever learned to read and
if freedom ever came, I would not read that part of the
Bible.[49]

—Nancy Ambrose, Howard Thurman's formerly enslaved grandmother

We poor creatures have need to believe in God, for if
God Almighty will not be good to us some day, why were
we born? When I heard of his delivering his people from
bondage, I know it means poor Africans.[50]

—Polly, a formerly enslaved woman, to her mistress

Reflection on Talking Book
WHITNEY WILKINSON ARRECHE

The name of the ship was Jesus, colloquially referred to as the
"Good Ship Jesus." This Jesus was built in Lübeck, Germany, and
came to be owned by Henry VIII. Elizabeth I gave permission in
1562 for John Hawkins to use it for a journey from Sierra Leone
to the Dominican Republic. This Jesus bore between three to five
hundred enslaved Africans. This Jesus was the beginning of overt
British involvement in the Transatlantic Slave Trade.

As far as I can tell, there was not a slave ship named Moses.

But, Jesus—that name served the purposes of hatred and subjection nicely. I am reminded of a workshop I once attended led by
the Minister for Racial Justice in the United Church of Christ, Rev.

49. Thurman, *Jesus and the Disinherited*, 31.
50. Callahan, *The Talking Book*, 83.

Dr. Velda Love. She began by unequivocally saying, "We do not follow the same Jesus."

So, the question is, whose Jesus do we follow? And, for that matter, whose Bible do we read?

As a white woman of progressive leanings, I hear many people who look and vote like me express outrage at the censorship of books deemed too subversive for public consumption. Memes of Nazi book burnings fill my newsfeed and are met with impassioned cries of never again. This matters. And this is also symptomatic of a white women's feminism that pays attention to subjection from a safe distance and not within our own genealogical and economic connections to the enslavement of African people here, and the continued economies of subjection affecting African diasporic people. This particular activism also doesn't often meet the book many of us hold most dear: the Bible. While there may be attention to how this book has hurt women's bodies, those women are usually white. There's little engagement with how the words in this book have been used to steal African people, racialize them as other, force them into labor, and call all of this a blessing and mandate of God.

When enslaved Africans were taught the Bible, it was a heavily redacted version. The Exodus was removed, as was most of the Old Testament. References to racial unity disappeared, as did the entire book of Revelation. Scripture was butchered by white supremacy, leaving only what was good news to white people. Masters and pastors charged with the spiritual "care" of enslaved persons instead leaned heavily upon Paul. This is why Howard Thurman's grandmother would no longer read Pauline epistles. Scripture was also forced into a sort of smiling compliance: writings about slaves obeying masters were elevated to supra-canonical status. This slave Bible was unequivocal when it came to obedience and submission. Dr. Allen Dwight Callahan names the Bible "the poison book" for this reason. But Callahan claims that the poison was also the antidote, writing, "As both curse and cure, slavery's children would distill antidotes for the toxic texts of the Bible and make those texts their own."[51]

In the hush harbors, enslaved Africans taught one another a different Bible. They pointed to and created a new reality. Through story-songs, they learned of an Exodus where the liberation of enslaved people was God's primary concern. As Noel Erskine writes, "Down in the hush arbors, enslaved people would sing, 'Go down Moses, way down in Egypt's land. Tell old pharaoh to let my people go.' Enslaved persons learned early to gather to worship and strategize under the cover of night or under the cover of the woods where a redefinition of their status took place."[52] Under cover, hidden in plain sight for those with eyes to see, they learned of prophets who called out greed, especially money gained through unjust means. They learned of a Jesus who was very different from that so-called "good" ship; a Jesus who, like his mother, cast down the mighty from their thrones, filled the hungry with good things, and sent the rich away empty (Luke 1:46–55). They learned of a fire-in-the-bones Spirit poured out on all flesh, even and especially enslaved flesh (Acts 2:1–21). They learned of a Revelation of all that is wrong being turned upside down, in a flourishing garden not tended by enslaved labor (Revelation 22). This talking book was the antidote to slavery's prooftexted shouting.

That antidote is still sorely needed in a church and theology that continues to perpetuate the prooftexted lies of white supremacy. These lies come in many forms. They appear as an over-representation of Paul's words, particularly his words about submission and obedience. They also appear as ideas that the New Testament renders the Old obsolete, or worse, evil. I addressed some of these lies when I was a teaching assistant for an Old Testament course. On the last day of the course, one of the professors asked some of the teaching assistants to share their biblical hermeneutics regarding the Hebrew Bible. This is academic jargon for "how do you choose to read and interpret Scripture?" I had not planned on speaking. But sometimes you have a fire-in-the-bones

51. Callahan, *The Talking Book*, 40.
52. Erskine, *Plantation Church*, 134.

moment. I found myself at the microphone speaking to the class of Master of Divinity students. Informed by all I've learned being a part of curating *Liberating Church*, I told them that white-supremacist plantation churches, on the whole, amputated the Old Testament from the Bible. The Hebrew Bible represented a threat to the master's theological and physical power exercised over his human property. I told these eager divinity students that if we only read, teach, and preach the New Testament, particularly when we heavily center the writings attributed to Paul, we are perpetuating a plantation church ethic of Scripture. If, instead, we center narratives of liberation and survival, refusing to sanitize Jesus and refusing to spiritualize physical freedom, we get closer to the hush harbor. We get closer to the power of the Talking Book. We get closer to what can actually be called gospel—good news.

We do not all follow the same Jesus.

We also do not all read the same Bible.

Whose Jesus? The Jesus co-opted by empire in whom enslaved humans were literally held captive? Or the Jesus of the hush harbor, whose compassion—shared suffering—meant that heaven itself was shaken by the injustices of earth, and resolved to do something about it?

Whose Bible? The whited-out version that perpetuates colonial power? Or the Bible of the hush harbor that didn't need fancy binding or ordered preaching to make it legitimate, but rather was woven out of song and sweat and stolen time? The Bible that proclaimed a master God lording over captive bodies and souls, or the Bible that proclaimed a God relentlessly leading people to freedom in all its forms?

It is not enough for United States Christians in our time to say we follow Jesus. It is not enough to be woke if our wokeness doesn't ever meet our theology, or our sacred text. It is not enough for us to cling to our enlightened NRSVs, oblivious to the stains of colonial power and slavery that haunt those pages still. Now is the time to be very, very clear about exactly which Jesus we follow, and exactly which Bible we read. Now is the time to listen—and speak back to—the Talking Book.

The Six Communities

~

NEW BIRTH COMMUNITY AME CHURCH

New Birth Community African Methodist Episcopal Church (NBC) started as a mission community in June 2003. Based in Greensboro, NC, the mission of New Birth Community AME Church is to: "equip God's people with knowledge of the Word of God in order that they may be effective witnesses for Christ and lead more fruitful, productive and joyful lives; through good clean practical application of the rightly divided Word." NBC does not have a permanent building. Instead, they rent space for Sunday collective worship from another congregation. NBC spends most of its time in ministry outside of the Sunday gathering in the community. Rev. Kathy A. Merritt is the pastor of NBC. Membership of NBC is a serious matter. To join NBC is understood as "marrying" the community, every member becomes part of a spiritual family and takes responsibility for the community and its ministries. The membership and culture of NBC demonstrate a commitment to families and women's leadership. In many ways, as a middle-aged Black woman, Rev. Merritt embodies the strong maternal culture of NBC. NBC provides intentional accountability and support for its members to be cared for in a holistic way—mind, body, and spirit—so that every member can show up ready to serve and worship. NBC engages in a variety of intergenerational ministries in the wider community such as art and theater, sports, community gardens, and contributing to local non-profit organizations that serve low-income neighbors. Consistent with their commitment to the whole person, the NBC Sunday morning worship experience is focused on participation, community, and the full-range of emotional wellness. From the music to the sermon, the Sunday worship gathering is intellectually and emotionally accessible to all.

Kinfolk/Elders/Ancestors

Jarena Lee, Fannie Lou Hamer, Miriam (Moses' older sister)

Strongest Marks

From the time you enter the parking lot until you find your seat in the sanctuary, NBC embodies hospitality and welcome. You're sure to receive ten or more hugs before you leave the community on a Sunday. Every aspect of the service is intentional in creating a joy-filled atmosphere for everyone to feel welcome and ready to praise and worship God in community, attesting to the strong presence of Joy Unspeakable. NBC does not have bulletins or programs. In place of them, NBC powerfully reflects the principle of Ubuntu through creating an environment where visitors feel safe, and seen, and like part of the family. NBC embodies All God's Children Got Shoes because everyone plays a role. It is not immediately clear to a visitor who is "in charge" because from the kids to elders, the multitude of people are each playing a role rather than simply sitting in pews.

All God's Children Got Shoes

We focus on a ministry partnership. So we don't have the thought that the church belongs to the pastor, it belongs to us. And so we're responsible for it. We're responsible for the feel of it. We're responsible for what happens in it.

So it's not the traditional model of the pastor carrying it all. That's not what we subscribe to.

—Jessica Stukes, member-leader

Pastor preaches on the floor because there's not a division. A couple of weeks ago we had tag-team preaching by people who are not ordained, by people who don't have a Master of Divinity, because the Word is in everyone. The delivery may be different, but everybody has a Word so it reinforces our sense of equality.

—Dr. Allyson A. Alston, member-leader

Joy Unspeakable

To me, at NBC mystery looks like no bulletins. We purposely don't have bulletins. Because you don't know what's going to happen and in what order. You don't know who's going to offer the word that day. You don't know who's going to pray. That's the mystery of NBC. You never know what you're going to get when you walk in.

—Dr. Allyson A. Alston, member-leader

Pastor really listens to the spirit . . . We may have prepared something, but if we come in and the feel of the house is something different, then we're doing something different. Because our job is to meet the needs of the people where they are on that Sunday morning. And what we prepared a week ago may not be what the people need that morning. So we switch and we ask God to do what we know he's capable of doing. We've already prepared and we know he honors that. So then we just move in his Spirit.

—Jessica Stukes, member-leader

Ubuntu

Our job is to save souls. And so it's my job to be in tune enough to know what chemistry can build the best team to do that. And sometimes you bring things into a place too soon and it disrupts the chemistry. And so then the team members are not able to do what they're supposed to do because of the disruption. Well, I'm building a team, the New Zion that could save the souls to build a better place to live.

—Rev. Kathy A. Merritt

There are no smoke screens here. There is accountability. I think that's the biggest thing that would probably scare people away. The accountability of ownership and investment, not only investment in NBC, but mostly investment in people. We as a community work with people to become who God has called them to be. We're not gonna work more than you're willing to work.

—Jessica Stukes, member-leader

We provide every member an IEP, an Individual Educational Plan. But what we do is put a plan together for your life. So it's an encouragement plan, more or less.

—Rev. Kathy A. Merritt

～

MISSION HOUSE

Mission House is a church rooted in the East Spencer, Salisbury, and Greater Rowan county area of North Carolina. They began as an informal but committed band of Jesus followers in 2011 and became a formal church in 2015. Their mission is "to mobilize an army of love for the good of our neighborhood and city." This army's "cadences" are "spirit-led creativity," "gospel innovation," "kingdom hospitality," "deep learning," and "city-wide renaissance." Said another way, Mission House is a Spirit-animated force for justice, healing, radical welcome of neighbors, theological depth, and artistic and cultural expression. Mission House preaches a liberative Gospel with an African-centered hermeneutic. Its worship gathering style could be summed up as store-front Afro-Pentecostalism, meets contemplative spirituality, meets the justice-oriented preaching of the prophetic Black Church. The church's leadership structure is egalitarian, and requirements for leadership are not based on age, gender, sexuality, etc. People of all ages lead in various capacities—from preaching, to singing, to community organizing work, to the arts. Membership, or as they call it, being a "missioner," is fluid and non-traditional. As co-pastor Anthony Smith put it:

> You become a "missioner" simply by participating in the mission. I know that's kind of loose but I've learned—if I can get technical—we are a "center set" community not a "bounded set" community. Most churches are a bounded set. You're not a part of their community unless you dot all your I's and cross all your T's. For us it's about . . . proximity. For me that's a part of discipleship. You [are] being brought into the movement.

Kinfolk/Elders/Ancestors

Ella Baker, Apostle Annie Rice, Oscar Romero, Harriet Tubman, John Perkins

Strongest Marks

Mission House's strongest marks were Ubuntu, Joy Unspeakable, and North Star. The spirit of Ubuntu is very tangible at Mission House. Their communal life is characterized by a deep sense of intimacy and mutuality. It is very apparent that "missioners" see themselves as being bound together and responsible for each other's healing and flourishing. There is a commitment to show up for one another, protect one another, and call one another higher. Being that almost one hundred percent of their Black members come from Pentecostal/charismatic backgrounds, the mark of Joy Unspeakable is second nature. Mission House has a vibrant and dynamic life with and in the Spirit. There are times when the power of God hits their gatherings and the "order of service" is thrown out as people prophesy, lay hands on each other for healing, and speak in tongues. Lastly, Mission House is truly grounded in a North Star praxis. Mission House is always convening the broader community to scheme and dream for liberation. They are actively involved in various local struggles for justice. The resources of this spiritual community are constantly leveraged to provoke and sustain movement-building.

Ubuntu

There is a permission to feel the hurt here, and to be vulnerable. The permission to feel that pain and then the healing that came from knowing I had family surrounding me. This is a healing space. It comes through hugs, prayer, laying on hands. It feels like we're in tune with each other whether it's on Sunday or another day.

—Ash Love

Joy Unspeakable

We have . . . sort of ecstatic moments of worship that would lead to everything from . . . prophesying and laying hands on folks . . . We expect the spirit's activity when we gather, and we expect it to not be something that can be planned.

—Anthony Smith, co-pastor

North Star

We are a movement organization. It's not static, it's always dynamic.

—Anthony Smith, co-pastor

⌣

QC FAMILY TREE

QC Family Tree, founded in 2005 and based in the historically Black neighborhood of Enderly Park in Charlotte, NC, is a faith-rooted hospitality house and community development organization. They describe themselves as a village of abundance that creates "spaces where everyone can thrive." The core practices to build this village include: immersive listening and learning, asset-based community development, relationship building, and incarnational ministry. The staff of QC Family Tree see themselves as artists, cultural organizers that help their village "to tell a different story about the world" rooted in imagination and change. The programmatic ministries of QC Family tree are rooted in discipleship and include affordable housing, youth development, and abundance lab workshops and retreats. QC Family Tree's current leadership includes Greg and Helms Jarrell, a white couple that founded the organization, and staff community cultivator Shamaiye Haynes. At the time of our interviews cultural organizer Hannah Hasan, and youth director Kayla Pinson, both non-Christian Black women, and a host of interns were on staff. The membership of the community includes neighborhood youth and their families, elders in the neighborhood, long-time and newer neighbors, and many volunteers, often from outside of the neighborhood that are members of local churches in the area.

Kinfolk/Elders/Ancestors

Clarence Jordan, Dorothy Day, Nina Simone, James Baldwin, Howard Thurman

Strongest Marks

From long-standing rhythms such as the weekly neighborhood meal to innovative projects such as a tiny school to respond to

55

working families' needs with virtual public schooling caused by the COVID-19 pandemic, QC Family Tree deeply embodies Ubuntu through their shared life together of mutual care among staff, neighbors, and volunteers. QC Family Tree models what it means to Stay Woke in many ways: the Jarrells' consistently educating white folks about the history of white supremacy and redistributing their resources to Black staff, youth, and neighbors; hiring staff from religiously diverse backgrounds and creating a welcoming spiritual environment for staff and neighbors to explore. Their work providing affordable housing and developing revolutionary youth leaders demonstrates QC Family Tree's commitment to building a new world pointing toward the North Star.

North Star

Is it even possible to have church in a way that is liberative given the current container or does the container just need to be demolished?

—Helms Jarrell

The organization has changed the way that I look at economics. I now look at economics in terms of what is needed to sustain communities.

—Hannah Hasan, former staff cultural organizer

Stay Woke

Brother Greg and Ms. Helms have taken everything, all the people that they know, all the relationships that they have, all the power that they have and tossed it on the table for us to have access to. That is what reparations looks like.

—Kayla Pinson, former staff youth director

We're always coming back to the Christian story. That theme of escape from and resistance to empire, that's always coming back.

—Greg Jarrell

Ubuntu

But every day when I walk to the store half the people are on drugs. I say, what's up? I say, "Bro, you having a good day. You good, you got everything you need? Alright bet! We're having a community meal down here, we got free food. Come down." It's never a closed door. Cause if you close the door, who did God close the door on? Jesus was with the thieves.

—Kayla Pinson, former staff youth director

A lot of members give time, car driving, meal provisions, babysitting, dog walking . . . toilet paper, you know, like all those kinds of things. So it's just organized very differently and it's a lot less organized. I think we're streamlined and we are not, it's not chaos over here, but we don't have committees. We don't have bulletins. We don't have all that stuff the churches have. The immersiveness is like nothing else.

—Helms Jarrell

~

GOOD NEIGHBOR MOVEMENT

The Good Neighbor Movement (GNM) is a network of contemplative activist groups. Founded in 2017, GNM has a once-a-month collective Sunday worship service. They deploy most of their resources to support the worship and activism that happens through small groups located in various neighborhoods throughout the city of Greensboro, North Carolina. The Good Neighbor Movement's mission is to be "a Black-led, multiracial, queer-affirming alternative spiritual community that is inspired by the life and ministry of Jesus to cultivate intentional relationships, work collaboratively, and pursue justice with diverse neighbors in Greensboro to create inclusive, local communities that are abundant, just, and whole." Their values are:

BELONG: How will we be loving and inclusive and demonstrate that we value our neighborhoods? How will we practice authenticity and care?

BE STILL: How do we develop the habits to be present to God within us, our neighbors, our enemies, and the world? How will we practice accountability and rootedness?

BECOME: How do we listen for what is needed to pursue transformation of ourselves, our neighborhoods, and city? How will we practice hospitality and solidarity?

BE BOLD: How will we take action, sacrifice, and speak truth to power to see this transformation realized? How will we practice justice and innovation?

Theologically, the Good Neighbor Movement is committed to an inclusive and liberationist reading of Scripture and they incorporate the wisdom and rituals of various religious and cultural traditions in their gatherings. For GNM, the Gospel equals "God is our neighbor." They are a leader-full space that believes all have something to offer and contribute to the life of the community and for the good of their city.

Kinfolk/Elders/Ancestors

Ella Baker, Septima Clark, Howard Thurman, Vincent Harding, Harriet Tubman, Martin Luther King Jr., Fannie Lou Hamer, Oscar Romero, Nelson Johnson, Alexia Salvatierra, adrienne maree brown, James Baldwin, Dietrich Bonhoeffer, John Wesley

Strongest Marks

GNM's strongest marks are Steal Away, North Star, and Ubuntu. This alternative spiritual community embodies the ethics and orientation of "Steal Away" by refusing to be built off of "branding" and "visibility." Instead, they create and cultivate discreet communities of presence that offer respite from the traumas of white supremacy, heteropatriarchy, and the spiritual abuses of institutional churches. The Good Neighbor Movement has a beautiful commitment and practice of what they call "soul-full organizing." They are actively involved in mutual aid, coalition building, and grassroots political organizing around things like police brutality, voter suppression, housing justice, and workers rights. Lastly, GNM's model of contemplative activist groups gives it a very strong practice of Ubuntu. People who are a part of these groups cultivate authentic relationships in specific neighborhoods. The sense of *place* undergirds their practices of care and covenant-keeping.

Steal Away

> So it's kind of like this healthy, ambiguous relationship [with other churches and the wider community] that they see that we're about something and that we want to connect with the larger community in a social justice way and they see a lot of people of color and women and queer folks connected to us, but since we don't have a building and we're not like doctrinaire, trying to proselytize, I think we have a sort of you know ambiguous presence in a lot of contexts, which like I said, I think is good, actually.
>
> —member-leader

> We have a city village group in a neighborhood called Old Asheboro . . . and we meet in homes and we also have a community garden in the neighborhood where we'll meet sometimes for monthly gatherings, but the weekly gatherings are in neighborhood homes and we switch off who hosts within the group.
>
> —Kelly Florence

> I want to emphasize that it was an organic development . . . it was maybe non-traditional, but as a local, independent business owner, a woman of color, and then having someone invite me to a meeting, it was just sort of a natural, organic development in terms of having this womxn-autonomous spiritual group meeting at my shop.
>
> —member-leader

North Star

listening in an authentic way has produced some meaningful authentic community ministry . . . whether it is working in gardens, involved in issue campaigns, doing get out the vote, you know, electoral kind of things . . . listening to folks has also meant taking the risk of putting an idea out there or sharing a concern and it not being what people actually wanted to do. So I can't tell you how many times I've knocked doors and I've followed up and done one on one meetings with neighbors thinking it was going to be one thing . . . Community ministry and social justice is always evolving. And sometimes it means what I thought was a priority, or what was a priority for me is not a priority for other folks . . .

—Brandon Wrencher

I'm riffing off of our ancestors, but like, none of us can be truly free until we're all free and that freedom looks different depending on where we stand and what we've benefitted from.

—Erica Wrencher

Ubuntu

I think a lot of it has to do with telling stories and also prioritizing feelings and respite as the primary function of church rather than trying to get something else out of it. Like it's not about checking boxes, it's not about conforming or fitting one mode of Christianity, but how do we create sites of hope and healing and action using these words from this ancient text that can be applicable today.

—Indhira Udofia

[GNM] is intentionally a space where we have parameters by which people can come into a closer walk with each other and understand what it is to share a life together. So, in our specific city village we have covenants that we decide we will follow together. So in those covenants it spells out how we are choosing to live and choosing to follow Jesus together.

—Erica Wrencher

~

GREENWAY COMMUNITY

Greenway Community had its first gathering on December 10th, 2017. This off-the-grid, non-501(c)(3), and unnamed community of folks generally meets at the edge of the Northeast ward of Winston-Salem in the home of one of its participants. Though there is no formalized "mission statement" or set of "values," the collective is rooted in the holistic liberationist values of the Black Radical Church Tradition. Demographically, this hush harbor is seventy percent Black, twenty-five White, and five percent Brown. Because a good portion of the group are community organizers and activists, their external ministry practices generally involve supporting broader local movements for healing justice. They believe in the priesthood of believers and are generally leader-full without any official titles or membership process. Belonging to the community is simply understood as participating regularly in their gatherings and committing to loving God, each other, and your neighbor— especially the oppressed. They have hush harbor gatherings twice a month on Sunday afternoons and have a weekly time of prayer and meditation.

Kinfolk/Elders/Ancestors

Howard Thurman, Harriet Tubman, Martin King, and Fannie Lou Hamer

Strongest Marks

The Greenway Community initially gathered out of an exodus of several community leaders and neighbors from traditional multiracial and white church spaces, attesting to the centrality of Steal Away to this community's existence. Rather than trying to quickly formalize the community with a name (Greenway Community is a "place-holder"), building, and so forth, this rag-tag group of rebels continued to embrace the organic and informal nature of stealing away by gathering in homes and in the streets. Most of the community's ministries are activism and mutual aid demonstrating the priority that organizing for the North Star has in the community. Because the community was formed from a group of persons exiting harmful spaces, from the beginning, the Greenway Community was clear about its theological and political analysis, having no tolerance for harmful attitudes, ideologies, and behaviors. Stay Woke is critical to the community's ongoing need for healing and growth.

Steal Away

We gather in our hood, in our neighborhood, in northeast Winston Salem, which is a historically oppressed, predominantly Black neighborhood, now increasingly Black and Brown. And so because we're Black centered, we think it is important to be in spaces that are in our communities and the Salt Box [community center] and our homes fit our commitment to gathering on the wrong side of the tracks.

—Terrance Hawkins

I was actually terrified of becoming "a thing." It's the best when it isn't a thing. It starts to feel terrifying when people are demanding titles, not demanding titles for themselves, but demanding it to have a label, of demanding more structure . . . it starts to freak me out when we start to become official. I like it when we're not fully clear.

—Allonda Hawkins

North Star

If there is somebody who is struggling to get rent paid we all collectively pitch in and help them pay it.

—Terrance Hawkins

Kids attend protests, too.

—Allonda Hawkins

Stay Woke

White people are not centered in any way, shape, or form. Us coming out of "multicultural spaces" and racial reconciliation paradigms where it basically still centers whiteness and this is like the total other end of the spectrum.

—Terrance Hawkins

Our church announcements were things that were happening in the community. Whether it had been a shooting, whether it had been a police killing, or whatever it was that was happening in the community, that was a part of our announcements.

—Allonda Hawkins

~

THE GATHERING

I see the ways that the black woman's body has been politicized itself. So there's no . . . Womanist work devoid of politics. So, being in a place that . . . welcomes and has a heart for social justice out in the community beyond the walls . . . it didn't begin as, you know, a church, it was doing the work.

—ministry partner, The Gathering

If there's any way to describe The Gathering—the nearly three-year-old Disciples of Christ Christian community in Dallas led by co-pastors Rev. Dr. Irie Lynne Session and Rev. Kamilah Hall Sharp—it is that they *do the work.* In their own words, "The Gathering exists to welcome people into community to follow Jesus, partner in ministry to transform our lives together, and to go create an equitable world." On Saturday nights they gather (in person and online) to worship together. What sets this community apart from so many Christian communities is that they exist for one purpose: to center and celebrate Black women preachers. Where so many Christian communities place Black women on the sidelines of their life and pulpit, The Gathering does the work of creating space for, listening to, and trusting Black women. The centering of the Black woman's experience that is so central to womanist theology is not only in the pulpit, though it is certainly there. So, too, is the Black woman centered in naming and sharing the pain of a politicized body; in celebrating the fullness and complexity of Black women's identities; in discovering women in Scripture and other Christian narratives that resonate with the Black women's experience; in decolonizing Christian thought and practice through unapologetic engagement with the witness of Black women. The Gathering is clear, though, that this work is not only for women to do. "It is about women and men working together to dismantle the systemic structures that seek to oppress people."

Kinfolk/Elders/Ancestors

Sojourner Truth, Alice Walker, Chanequa Walker-Barnes, Emilie Townes, Katie Geneva Cannon

Strongest Marks

The Gathering embodies the Talking Book in every service where the gathered community is invited to literally talk back to the sermon. They embody Stay Woke through engagement with participation in the Dallas Black Clergy for Safety Equity and Justice, calling out police brutality, economic inequity, and systemic racism. They embody Sankofa by reaching back to their Black women ancestors for wisdom and courage in the present moment. In so many other ways, as a twenty-first-century hush harbor, The Gathering does the work of meeting the intersectional pains of racism, sexism and homophobia with the courageous healing that comes when Black women preach.

Talking Book

We were interested in just creating a space where we could share Womanist preaching with Dallas.

—Rev. Dr. Irie Lynne Session

For me and for my being, for who it is that I am and what I bring to the space, [The Gathering] allows an opportunity for me as a black woman and some other black women to get the opportunity to preach. We don't get that opportunity for traditional churches because we're still minimized or obstructed.

—Rev. Winner Laws

Stay Woke

. . . not only did we preach about it, but Kamilah and I are a part of the Dallas Black Clergy team, black clergy who are committed together to meeting with city hall, to have individual meetings with each council person to do the action work . . . We're actually out there doing justice, doing social justice as well as preaching.

—Rev. Dr. Irie Lynne Session

Sankofa

I also love it that often in our preaching and prayer we talk about the ancestors. I like to believe we reach back and get the teachings of our ancestors and that's the things that we try to teach [about them], and honor them.

—Rev. Kamilah Hall Sharp

Conclusions

THANK YOU FOR TAKING this journey with us. Taking a walk through the eight liberating church marks has been a faith-fueled, imaginative task. We are doing the work of *Sankofa*, reaching back to retrieve what our ancestors have left behind for us. Guided by our *North Star*, we are being led into a new world, yet a world that has been with us for centuries. This world is one in which *All God's Children Got Shoes*, we all have equal say into how we live, move, and have our being. The Spirit of God sustains and enlivens us with *Joy Unspeakable*. The *Talking Book*, the Word of God, is one that speaks to us and we talk back, raising our consciousness of ourselves, the world around us, and the changes we want to realize. The work ahead of us demands that we *Stay Woke* and remain committed to seeing the liberative realities of Heaven be felt and made known on Earth.

The moment that we now find ourselves in requires that we forge ahead together. The marks *North Star, Ubuntu, Talking Book* and *Steal Away* were the most prominent within the six communities we studied. This is evidence of the need for our collective life together, for ring shouts and Spirit-dances and sacred story-songs revealing and building a new world, for mutually made and maintained spaces to gather that are hidden outside of the gaze of dominating institutional forces where we can freely practice the biblical and humane acts of communal living rooted in interdependence. In our post-COVID context, further complicated and exacerbated by political and social upheaval, we desperately need a way of life in our communities that links heart to heart and struggles collectively toward real cultural and political change.

The principle of **North Star** summons us to:

> To be a people that embody, in our collective life together, a prefigurative community rooted in love, justice and mercy. To be a people that work collectively to build a new world in the places we inhabit.

The principle of **Ubuntu** demands that:

> We must know and believe that our well-being is tied up with the well-being of the people in closest proximity to us, and to all those that are oppressed.

The principle of **Talking Book** challenges us to interrogate:

> Whose Bible?. . .The Bible that proclaimed a master God lording over captive bodies and souls, or the Bible that proclaimed a God relentlessly leading people to freedom in all its forms?

The principle of **Steal Away** teaches us that:

> The appeal of the hush harbors was both liturgical and political. Like the liberation they sought from the plantation economy, the hush harbor was a site to liberate Christianity in service to the well-being and freedom dreams of enslaved Africans.

We are experiencing the shrinking of the commons, spaces where our shared life together (politically, socially, culturally, economically) have unraveled due to hyper-individualism, the defunding and privatizing of public goods, and the deep greed that motivates and mechanizes our institutions. In the belly of this white-supremacist Empire, we are waiting for new hush harbors. While we are waiting, we also see the Spirit creating liberating spaces of refuge and resistance. This is a *kairos* moment, a moment that requires presence, that demands action.

We lift up the legacy of hush harbors as embodied in present-day liberating churches. We resist the shrinking of the commons by cultivating alternative spaces for liberation, wholeness, and humanity. We host space for lamenting the emotional, physical, and spiritual effects of resisting and experiencing racism, the militarization of law enforcement, and policy violence directed at the poor.

These eight marks of liberating churches offer us a window, a kind of "holy seeing" into the living petitions of our ancestors. We are the evidence of things hoped for by this great cloud of witnesses. The Spirit hovers over our shared life, infusing us with everlasting revolutionary power. This power manifests itself in the lives of ordinary people radicalized by the extraordinary vision of the New Jerusalem, a place in which there is equal flourishing fueled by love.

We steal away into new worlds hidden in plain sight, together. May God go with us. May we go with God.

Litany of Affirmations
and Intentions

And now these three remain:

Faith

Don't ask what the world needs. Ask what makes you come alive, and go do it. Because what the world needs is people who have come alive.

—Howard Thurman

You are a light. You are the light. Never let anyone—any person or any force—dampen, dim or diminish your light. Study the path of others to make your way easier and more abundant. Lean toward the whispers of your own heart, discover the universal truth, and follow its dictates.

—John Lewis

Keep going. If you want a taste of freedom, keep going. I had reasoned this out in my mind; there was one of two things I had a right to, liberty or death; if I could not have one, I would have the other; for no man should take me alive. Never wound a snake; kill it.

—Harriet Tubman

Hope

When I think of music, I think of music in its totality, complete. From the lowest blues to the highest symphony, you know, so what I'd like to do is exemplify each style of as many periods as I can possibly do.

—Donny Hathaway

My music is the spiritual expression of what I am—my faith, my knowledge, my being . . . When you begin to see the possibilities of music, you desire to do something really good for people, to help humanity free itself from its hang-ups.

—John Coltrane

Color is life, or a world without color appears to us as dead. Colors are the children of light, and light is their mother. Light . . . reveals to us the spirit and living soul of the world, through colors. The colors of the rainbow and the Northern Lights soothe and elevate the soul. The rainbow is accounted as a symbol of peace.

—Alma Woodsey Thomas

and Love

Love takes off the masks we fear we cannot live without and know we cannot live within.

—James Baldwin

Love is or it ain't. Thin love ain't love at all.

—Toni Morrison

Love recognizes no barriers. It jumps hurdles, leaps fences, penetrates walls to arrive at its destination full of hope.

—Maya Angelou

I have decided to stick with love. Hate is too great a burden to bear.

—Martin Luther King Jr.

but the greatest of these is Love.

Throw it away
Throw it away
Give your love, live your life
Each and every day.
And keep your hand wide open

And let the sunshine through
'Cause you can never lose a thing
If it belongs to you.

—Abbey Lincoln

Epilogue
A Love Note to Future Hush Harbors

You ARE ALREADY BUT not yet. You inhabited the prayers, chants and ring shouts of your ancestors. Dear ones please remember you are surrounded by a cloud of witnesses that stole away to the North Star. To distant places and spaces that exist both geographically and in the collective imaginations of those running for the freedom line. Whose earthly home was an abode of unspeakable joy amid hostile death-dealing powers. You are tabernacled in their praise. The breathed seeded prayers they gave the earth with their mouths were the seeds of this moment. You are the amen to their lament, shouts and dancing. Stay vigilant and awake. Remember you are hemmed in by a power greater than the idols of this faltering Empire. Greater than the boot of oppression. You have each other. We are because you are. May you sing with tongues of fire. May you go back and retrieve the treasures from the past. May you tarry till you catch on fire to light the ancient way for future generations. May the icon of Scripture continue to talk to you the way it talked to our ancestors. Gifting them with liberating, subversive and revolutionary stories and revelations of the sacred that is our inheritance. May you grab hold together the ropes of God to bring down the New Jerusalem, that beloved community that is breaking forth. May your faithful and fruitful existence be a divine provocation. Shake the heavens until the crooked places are made straight and high places made low. We are not waiting for a new saint Benedict to rescue the Imperial project from its own self-destructive idols as others long for. We summon the multitude of Baby Suggs.[1] You are here and we await your full arrival, to lead us and guide us into love of God, our bodies, this earth, and our communities.

Ashe and amen.

---

1. Baby Suggs was a hush harbor preacher ordained by the people and the Spirit, a Black woman, a healer, an organizer from Toni Morrison's book *Beloved.*

Data Summary

Our team used the eight marks to design questions to administer surveys to members and facilitate interviews with clergy and lay leaders of these six Black faith communities in the South. Fifty-eight members completed the survey and we completed interviews with ten clergy and fifteen lay leaders of the different communities. There were many patterns to our ethnographic research with these communities. Many of the marks occurred frequently throughout every community. The marks that were represented the most in interviews and corroborated by surveys were: Ubuntu, Steal Away, Talking Book, and North Star. We developed several themes (phrase codes) for each mark to represent the diversity of interview responses. The graphs in the next section depict the frequency of these themes to indicate the different ways that a mark was expressed in a community.

For Ubuntu, the themes Accountability and Support and Trust and Intimacy were the most frequent in interviews. Other Ubuntu themes were Healing and Wholeness and Intergenerational. These themes were less frequent but were also consistently present within each community. Over one-hundred occurrences of Ubuntu themes emerged throughout interviews. This was the most of all of the marks. Member surveys reflect the strong emphasis on Ubuntu in interviews. Ubuntu was embodied in these communities through advocating for each other, offering prayer, and showing up to be with one another during difficult times of life. Additionally, these communities demonstrated Ubuntu by their comfort with talking about personal challenges with each other.

The themes of Hidden in Plain Sight, Vetting, and Fugitivity appeared most frequently for Steal Away. Themes from Steal Away appeared over sixty times in interviews with leaders. Member surveys supported the strong presence of Steal Away as embodied by the communities through the places in which they gather—most communities do not gather in traditional churches but instead in homes, coffee shops, and borrowed spaces. Also, many communities have collaborative relationships with longer standing churches. Through the use of their buildings or materials, established churches provide needed support to these younger faith communities. Steal Away was expressed at Good Neighbor Movement in the focus on personal and social liberation and that the distributed and discreet groups offer sanctuary for oppressed members from all the trauma and suffering they experience in their daily lives.

For Talking Book, the themes of Resistance, Biblical Lens, and Many Voices were frequently represented in interviews. Though Talking Book did not emerge as prominently in the interviews as Ubuntu, the mark appeared just over fifty times. Member surveys depicted that Talking Book was demonstrated through an emphasis on education, especially in learning about freedom and social justice in the Bible. Additionally, many communities engaged in shared or collaborative preaching with an emphasis on woman-centered preaching. At Mission House, Talking Book is present through the community's emphasis on liberation within Scripture.

The themes of Soul Work, Advocacy and Public Witness, and Awareness and Education were very strongly represented for Stay Woke through interviews. This mark was embodied through centering Blackness, and hearing, praying, and learning about social justice and slavery within the community. At The Gathering, Stay Woke was present in the way intersectional analysis of oppression is a priority, which creates space for people from diverse backgrounds to be welcome and seen in the community.

North Star was another mark that appeared most frequently in the communities. The themes of North Star occurred just over fifty times in interviews. In particular, the North Star themes of Beyond a Building, Escape and Protest, and Full Humanity were the most frequent. With Mission House, North Star was present in the community's commitment to political engagement with police brutality and voter suppression as well as in the community's celebration of the arts. With the Good Neighbor Movement, North Star was expressed in how the community provided sanctuary, hospitality, and mutual solidarity for one another. Each spiritual community cultivated North Star into their communities as a commitment and dedication to engaging in practices of resisting existing political structures and innovating alternative structures that meet immediate needs, all in service to building a new world.

In conclusion, Ubuntu, Steal Away, Talking Book and North Star were the most prominent marks in interviews, and supported by the results of member surveys. We observed patterns such as centering Blackness, a fluidity between formal and informal leadership structures, consistent direct relationships, accessible and collaborative preaching, providing gathering places that cultivate belonging and welcome, and mutual solidarity. Additionally, each of the communities demonstrated a focus on healing from trauma, interrogating larger social forces, incorporating the arts, and building community as a form of resistance. Even with the strong emphasis on these four marks, all of the eight marks were reflected in the communities through both interviews and surveys. Below find visual representations of our research results.

Interview Themes Defined

UBUNTU

Trust and Intimacy: sharing sensitive personal struggles
and joys with community members; spending time with
one another

Healing and Wholeness: acts of care for fellow
community members' well-being

Intergenerational: cultivating relationships and ministry
across age

Accountability and Support: holding one another to
standards of justice and growth and learning

STAY WOKE

Responding to Shared Pain: when a local and/or
national injustice hits the headlines, this is spoken to in
worship in a timely manner

Awareness and Education: consciousness-raising about
national and local issues of injustice, educating young
people

Soul Work: addressing injustices through healing internalized oppression and harm

Advocacy and Public Witness: engaging in electoral and issue-based political work

NORTH STAR

Story of the Spirit: that the future we are building is fundamentally Spirit-saturated world, is a prophecy, and is tied to the narrative of Scripture

Non-Linear: not needing bulletins or not being bound to an order of worship, seeing life and faith as process and movement oriented

Imagination: healing and justice include cultivating possibility, innovation, and futurism

Full Humanity: bodies and souls matter, feelings are welcomed and honored including hurt and anger

Escape and Protest: that acts of resistance to oppression and domination are essential for the whole community, including kids

Beyond a Building: not needing a constructed sanctuary, agile to not be bound to buildings and institutional limitations

ALL GOD'S CHILDREN GOT SHOES

Centering POC/Marginalized Voices: that those most on the margins in the community are given primacy of voice and leadership

Priesthood of All Believers: the Word is in and can come forth from everyone

Egalitarian Leadership: being leader-full, ownership and responsibility for the community by all who are part of the community; everyone contributes and plays a part; non-hierarchical leadership

STEAL AWAY

Agitate and Test: radical truth-telling, building discipline and rigor

Hidden in Plain Sight: being off-the-grid; gathering in a variety of spaces; betraying surveillance and performativity

Breaking Norms: disobeying unjust rules and laws

SANKOFA

Embodied/Rooted in Place: a ministry of practice that is fleshed out in specific places in specific ways

Reclaiming Ancestral Practices: carrying forward ancient ways of healing, knowing, and being from African ancestors, unapologetic Africanity in worship and practice

Telling the Stories: being a community of griots (story tellers), rooting ourselves in stories of those who came before us

Reaching Back: recovering buried history, un-silencing silenced stories

JOY UNSPEAKABLE

Non-Dualistic: not placing more importance over the body or spirit; able to see the sacred in all things including suffering

Mystery: beyond explanation, embrace of direct experiences of the sacred of "something more"

Holy Spirit Power: openness to the Spirit as opposed to being bound to strict order and outcomes; free to follow and feel the Spirit

TALKING BOOK

Memory and Story: the importance of the biblical text and preaching being about communal stories rather than explicating doctrines and beliefs

Biblical Lens: emphasis on hearing from God through the bible and not limiting the sources of authority in our lives to only our circumstances

Spirit and Mystery: the importance of the affective in preaching, that the community experiences feeling of healing and joy and connection to the sacred as a result of the preaching moment

Resistance: prioritizing the role of dissent and struggle against oppressors in the text and in preaching and teaching

Many Voices: preaching and teaching the biblical text from the perspective of the oppressed including the role of women, womanist interpretation, celebrating queerness, de-centering whiteness, de-weaponizing the Bible, and the perspective of the poor in the text

Graphs for Interviews and Surveys

EACH MARK IS FOLLOWED by a graph that depicts the quantitative results of interviews with leaders. Under this graph is a key that shows the number of times a theme occurred in interviews. Next are the graphs depicting the quantitative results of the member surveys. Following the graphs is a narrative summary of both the interviews and surveys.

UBUNTU
Interviews with Leaders

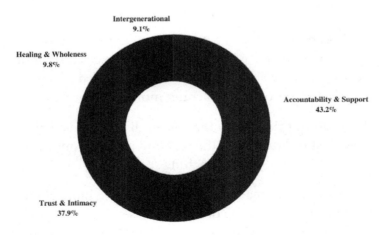

Intergenerational
9.1%

Healing & Wholeness
9.8%

Accountability & Support
43.2%

Trust & Intimacy
37.9%

Key:
Accountability & Support–57

Trust & Intimacy–50
Healing & Wholeness–13
Intergenerational–12

Member Surveys

Size of Spiritual Community:

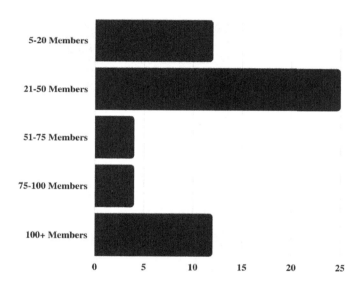

When life is hard, the spiritual community helps each other by offering:

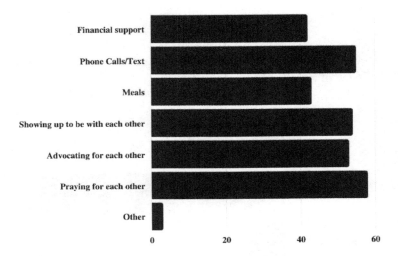

Comfortability talking about personal challenges and opportunities with members of their spiritual community:

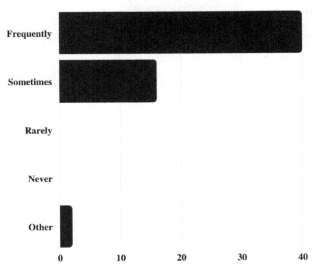

Summary

The themes of Accountability and Support as well as Trust and Intimacy were most reflective of Ubuntu in the interviews with leaders and clergy. The responses of members and volunteers supported these themes. Community members frequently feel comfortable talking about personal challenges with their spiritual community. Members and volunteers indicated many ways that care is expressed such as prayer, phone calls, showing up and advocating for one another, providing meals, and financial support. It is relevant that the strong presence of care is likely tied to these communities' commitment to being smaller in size or right-sized.

STAY WOKE
Interviews with Leaders

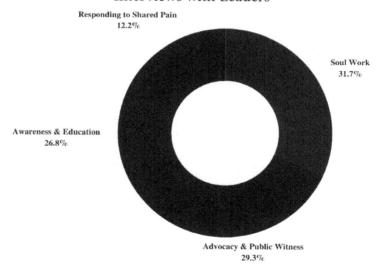

Responding to Shared Pain
12.2%

Soul Work
31.7%

Awareness & Education
26.8%

Advocacy & Public Witness
29.3%

Key:
Soul Work–13
Advocacy & Public Witness–12
Awareness & Education–5
Responding to Shared Pain–4

Member Surveys

How often the spiritual community hears, prays, and/or learns about slavery in the United States during a gathering:

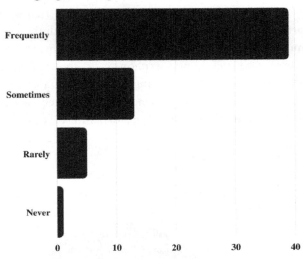

Forms of Diversity Present:

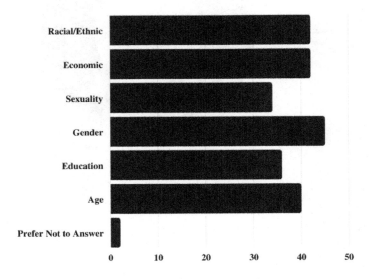

The spiritual community prioritizes Blackness while also creating space for people of all backgrounds and ethnicities to grow, learn and be challenged together:

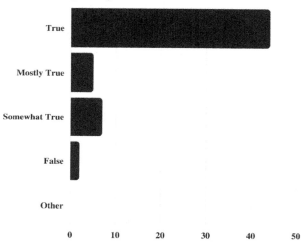

How often the spiritual community hears, prays, and/or learns about a social justice issue during a gathering:

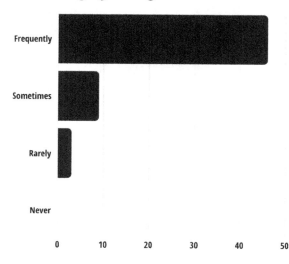

Summary

Stay Woke was most represented in the responses of leaders and clergy in the themes of Soul Work and Advocacy and Public Witness. Members and volunteers responded that they frequently learn about slavery and social justice issues during gatherings, and that their community centers Blackness while creating space for the presence of other forms of diversity such as gender, racial/ethnic, economic, sexuality, age, and educational background.

NORTH STAR
Interviews with Leaders

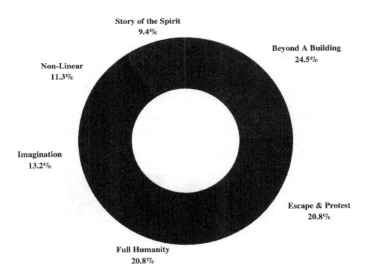

Story of the Spirit
9.4%

Beyond A Building
24.5%

Non-Linear
11.3%

Imagination
13.2%

Escape & Protest
20.8%

Full Humanity
20.8%

Key:
Beyond a Building–13
Full Humanity–11
Escape & Protest–11
Imagination–7
Non-Linear–6
Story of the Spirit–5

Member Surveys

Relationship between spiritual community & its gathering space:

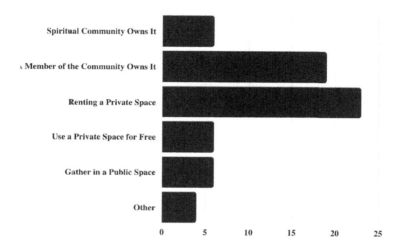

Ways in which the spiritual community actively betters the lives of the wider community:

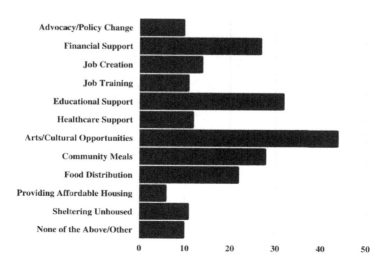

Summary

Leaders and clergy expressed the presence of North Star in their communities through the themes: Full Humanity, Escape and Protest, and Beyond A Building. Members and volunteers responded that North Star is demonstrated through their spiritual community through a variety of ministries and activism in the wider community including: arts and cultural opportunities, educational support, financial support, community meals and food distribution, providing safe spaces, food distribution, policy change, and healing practices. Members overwhelmingly responded that they either borrow or rent the buildings they use for ministry, which attests to the freedom they hold in relationship to buildings, that church is not defined by a building.

ALL GOD'S CHILDREN GOT SHOES
Interviews with Leaders

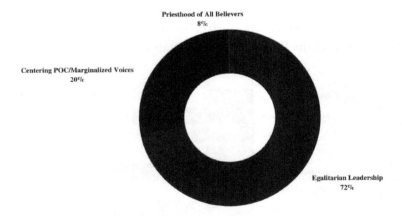

Priesthood of All Believers
8%

Centering POC/Marginalized Voices
20%

Egalitarian Leadership
72%

Key:
Egalitarian Leadership–18
Centering POC/Marginalized Voices–5
Priesthood of All Believers–2

Member Surveys
Who in the community makes important decisions:

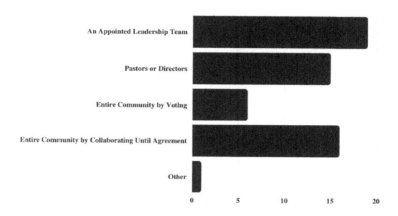

Eligibility for leadership:

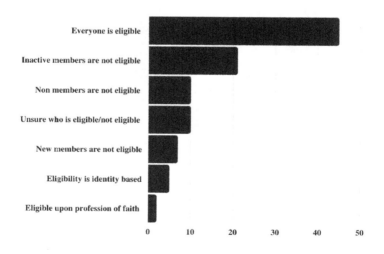

Summary

All God's Children Got Shoes was expressed in the themes

Egalitarian Leadership, appearing eighteen times or in seventy two percent of interviews with clergy and leaders, and Centering POC and Marginalized Voices, appearing in twenty percent of interviews. Members and volunteers of the six communities responded overwhelmingly that leadership and decision making is not reserved to one person or only those with official positions. Either an appointed leadership team, collaboration with the entire community, or pastors or directors are how decisions are made. In addition, members and volunteers indicated that mostly everyone in their spiritual communities is eligible for leadership.

STEAL AWAY
Interviews with Leaders

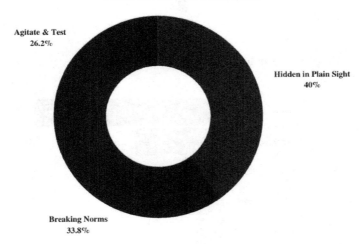

Agitate & Test
26.2%

Hidden in Plain Sight
40%

Breaking Norms
33.8%

Key:
Hidden in Plain Sight–26
Breaking Norms–22
Agitate & Test–17

Member Surveys
Gathering locations:

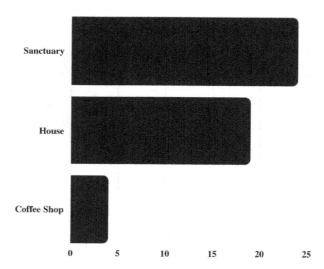

Describing the relationship with longer standing churches:

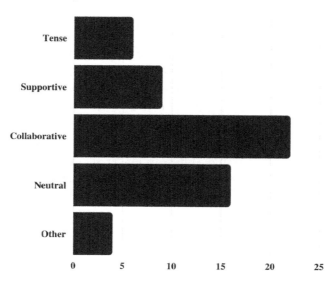

The ways in which members understand
how they came to belong to their spiritual
community:

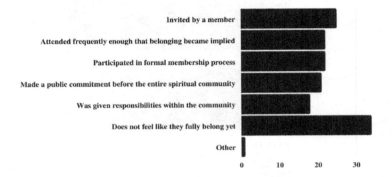

Summary

Steal Away was expressed in interviews with leaders and clergy through the themes Hidden in Plain Sight and Breaking Norms. In reference to gathering space, as many members and volunteers reflected that their communities gathered in a sanctuary as did those who gather in houses or coffee shops. This is revealing of the hidden way in which these communities gather outside of the traditional edifice of most churches. Even those who do gather in a sanctuary, the responses in North Star indicate that these congregations largely rent or use borrowed space, furthering the "on the move" style of stealing away. There were as many members and volunteers who responded that their church had a collaborative relationship with longer standing churches as those who responded that their church's relationship with longer standing churches is neutral or tense. Members and volunteers' responses to their sense of belonging to their churches was indicative of Steal Away, that there is intentionality to the process of becoming a committed part of the community. Many members stated they do not feel as though they fully belong yet and, in contrast, others stated they came to belong as they participated in formal membership processes, attended frequently, or made a public commitment before the entire spiritual community.

SANKOFA
Interviews with Leaders

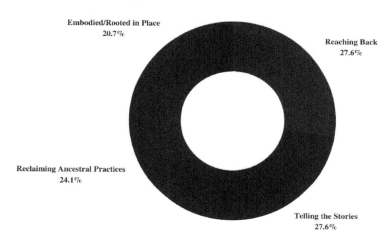

Embodied/Rooted in Place
20.7%

Reaching Back
27.6%

Reclaiming Ancestral Practices
24.1%

Telling the Stories
27.6%

Key:
Reaching Back–8
Telling the Stories–8
Reclaiming Ancestral Practices–7
Embodied/Rooted in Place–6

Member Surveys
African and Black culture, history, and ancestors are celebrated in the spiritual community:

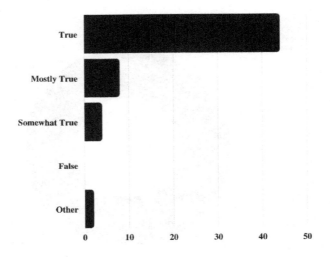

Summary

Sankofa was strongly represented throughout interviews with leaders and clergy through the themes Telling the Stories, Reaching Back, Reclaiming Ancestral Practices, and Embodied/Rooted in Place. Similarly, members and volunteers attested to the prominence of Sankofa as the overwhelming majority of them responded affirmatively that African/Black culture, history, and ancestors are celebrated in their community.

JOY UNSPEAKABLE
Interviews with Leaders

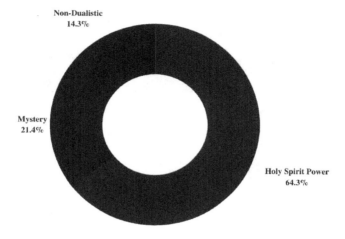

Non-Dualistic
14.3%

Mystery
21.4%

Holy Spirit Power
64.3%

Key:
Holy Spirit Power–9
Mystery–3
Non-Dualistic–2

Member Surveys

Members feel connected to a higher power when in the presence of their spiritual community:

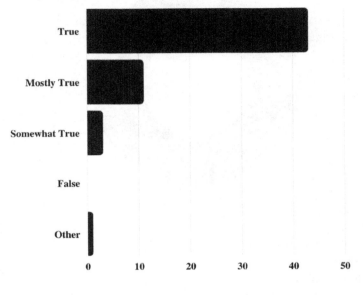

Summary

Holy Spirit Power is the most prominent theme that was expressed for Joy Unspeakable, appearing in sixty-four percent of responses from clergy and leaders. Attesting to the prominence of Joy Unspeakable in their communities, members and volunteers overwhelmingly answered that the following statement is true: "I frequently feel connected to a higher power when I'm with my spiritual community."

TALKING BOOK
Interviews with Leaders

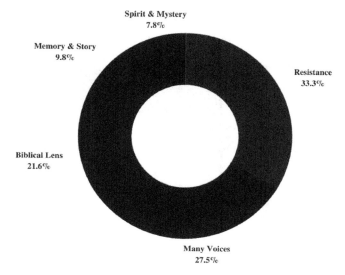

Spirit & Mystery
7.8%

Memory & Story
9.8%

Resistance
33.3%

Biblical Lens
21.6%

Many Voices
27.5%

Key:
Resistance–17
Many Voices–14
Biblical Lens–11
Memory & Story–5
Spirit & Mystery–4

Member Surveys

How often the spiritual community hears, prays, and/or learns about freedom/liberation/social justice in the bible or other sacred texts:

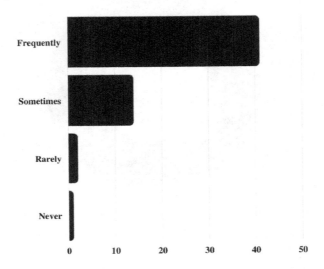

Summary

Talking Book was expressed in the responses of leaders and clergy through the themes of Resistance, Many Voices, and Biblical Lens. Members and volunteers expressed that they frequently heard, prayed, or learned about themes of freedom/liberation/social justice in the Bible and other sacred texts, attesting to the prominence of Talking Book in their spiritual communities. That both Many Voices and Resistance are grounded in a commitment to being leader-full, demonstrates the relationship between The Talking Book and All God's Children Got Shoes. Though the latter was not as prominent in the overall comments of leaders in interviews, it is clear that the value of non-hierarchical and full member participation is strongly tied to the role of preaching and communal engagement with Scripture.

Reflection Questions

A CHANGING LANDSCAPE QUESTIONS

1. How have you witnessed the pandemics of COVID-19 and anti-racist uprisings impact spiritual communities and faith leaders in your context?

2. "This moment has revealed that the way we have organized churches produces consumers not disciples, acquaintances not deep friendships, behavior modification not deep repentance, and volun-tourists not liberationists, flag-wavers not cross bearers, concubines of the state and not its conscience." What is your response to this assessment of the church's misalignment?

3. As a result of the changing landscape described here, what might change look like for your spiritual practice and the spiritual communities in your context?

CHURCH FROM THE MARGINS QUESTIONS

1. "Christianity in the United States has not always been beholden to white supremacy." How does this opening line contrast with how you have understood the history of Christianity, especially in the US?

2. How does Dr. Chanequa Walker-Barnes' perspective on giving up church compare to people you know (or yourself) who have left the church?

3. It's often said that progressive or social justice-focused congregations do not grow and are ineffective at reaching people through their faith. What is your response to this?

4. "Like the hush harbors, developing a vision of church from the margins is to develop decolonizing monastic missional communities, faith-rooted small groups on the fringes characterized by radical formation, friendship, and fierce revolution. In these spiritually and politically volatile times, equipping churches from the margins to go viral is critical for us to get free." What is your response to this assessment? Do you see this vision of church from the margins as vital for a more just and equitable future in the US and across the world?

UBUNTU REFLECTION QUESTIONS

1. How can your spiritual community share in mutual responsibility to care for the holistic needs of its members and the wider community?

2. How can your spiritual community live more fully into being intergenerational so that there is mutual respect, care, and growth among all ages?

3. How can your spiritual community build a culture of high trust and high mutual commitment so that accountability and forgiveness are regular practices between members?

STAY WOKE REFLECTION QUESTIONS

1. What distinguishes the "church in the wake" from other congregations?

2. What communal practices sustain and build our capacity to "stay woke"?

3. What gifts does a liberating church bring to bear in larger social movements?

4. What dangers are present for a church seeking to live into its calling as "the conscience of the state"?

NORTH STAR REFLECTION QUESTIONS

1. What is the North Star in your community?

2. How will you discern the journey towards that North Star? What tactics and practices will get you there?

3. What new social reality is the Spirit pushing you to help cultivate in your community?

4. Traveling to the North Star can be an arduous journey. What's in your backpack to help with the journey (self-care plan, community building practices, collective play plan, etc.)?

ALL GOD'S CHILDREN GOT SHOES REFLECTION QUESTIONS

1. Who around me isn't being valued or allowed to lead? Does my community's structure embody the belief that all have the capacity to lead and contribute meaningfully? Do we emphasize the idea of "the priesthood of all believers?" How is leadership and responsibility shared?

2. How can I expand the circle of voices that I'm reading or listening to and allowing to theologically shape my life?

3. How are we living into a world where we are not boxed in by borders and barriers, where we are free to walk all over God's Kin-dom now, both metaphorically and physically?

STEAL AWAY REFLECTION QUESTIONS

1. Is participation in your community dangerous and risky? If not, why? If so, how does your shared life together entail breaking the laws and customs of the dominant religious and societal systems?

2. Does your community practice holy deception? If not, why? If so, in what ways is your shared life together hidden in plain sight?

3. Are people exploring membership in your community vetted for political solidarity with the marginalized? If not, why? If so, what does it cost someone to be active in your community? How are they vetted and toward what political vision?

SANKOFA REFLECTION QUESTIONS

1. What are we at risk of losing within our rich African faith roots?

2. What must we "reach back and get" from our ancestors?

3. What is the danger of forgetting about the past contributions of queer and trans people of color to the church and society?

4. What are some ways queer and trans people of color are contributing to the present liberation of church?

5. What about the symbol of the Sankofa gives you hope for liberating churches? What gives you hope about the ways queer and trans people of color contribute to liberating churches?

JOY UNSPEAKABLE REFLECTION QUESTIONS

1. How does joy motivate the rhythms and decisions of your community?

2. When is joy unspeakable in your community?

3. Are there times when joy is a practice that interrupts business as usual in your community? Describe a time this was the case. Who benefited? Who was made uncomfortable?

4. What are concrete ways that you can cultivate joy as an act of resistance and pleasure in your community?

REFLECTION QUESTIONS

TALKING BOOK REFLECTION QUESTIONS

1. How might the sharing of Scripture in your community be more creative and egalitarian?

2. Is there an opportunity to respond to the preacher?

3. Does the word get proclaimed in many forms, by many people?

4. How has Scripture been poisonous to you or those in your community? (Remember that plantation Bibles also poisoned slaveholders with evil theology.)

5. What might biblical antidotes be?

THE SIX COMMUNITIES REFLECTION QUESTIONS

1. Which of the six communities is most familiar to you? Are there characteristics of the communities with which you're most familiar that differ from your experiences? Explain.

2. Which of the six communities challenges your experiences and beliefs about church? What about these communities is challenging and why?

3. What patterns and themes do you notice across the six communities?

4. What major differences exist between the six communities?

5. What are a few lessons or practices you can take from these communities into your own leadership and practice?

DATA SUMMARY QUESTIONS

1. Which data points really stood out to you and why?

2. How do the data and conclusions compare to the experiences of your spiritual community (or if you do not belong to a spiritual community, how do the data and conclusions reflect what you witness happening through spiritual communities in your context)?

Liberating Church Team

The Liberating Church team is encompassed by a diverse group of spiritual activists, community leaders, artists, researchers, ministers.[1] As leaders of different spiritual communities, the team came together to breathe life into this project. Each member of the team is dedicated to nurturing the wisdom of hush harbors into the present day. Here's a greater look into who each team member is:

BRANDON WRENCHER

Brandon is a minister, organizer, writer, teacher and facilitator. He works across the US within faith, education, and non-profit sectors at the intersections of decolonizing church, contemplative activism, and local presence to build beloved communities. As a serial innovator, Brandon with a team of friends and neighbors planted The Good Neighbor Movement, a multiracial, queer-affirming, Black-led alternative spiritual community organized as a network of contemplative activist groups, based in Greensboro, North Carolina. Brandon is an ordained elder in the Western North Carolina Conference of the United Methodist Church and serves on several local faith-based and social justice committees and boards. Brandon holds a BA in religion from UNC-Chapel Hill, a MDiv from North Park Theological Seminary, and completed post-graduate studies in theology and ethics from Duke Divinity School. He has

---

1. To contact any member of the Liberating Church team, visit liberating church.com.

written for *Sojourners, The Other Journal, Missio Alliance,* and other publications. Brandon is married to Erica, who is a cultural and social justice educator, and they have two elementary-aged sons. Brandon has served as the project director of Liberating Church, contributing his gifts of being a catalyst, group facilitation, passion for amplifying the stories of faith communities on the margins, and intellectual curiosity for charting fresh theological territory that impacts the church and society.

VENNEIKIA SAMANTHA WILLIAMS

Venneikia S. Williams is the current campaign manager for Media 2070, a media reparations project. As the former editorial and engagement director of a small nonprofit responsible for training other nonprofits, universities, and community members in justice-informed service and operations. As the former co-director of Faith for Justice, she invited people to participate in the radical, biblical-prophetic tradition by creating, coordinating, and promoting events to encourage public justice in St. Louis and beyond. Within her previous roles of worship leader, community organizer, and sociologist, Venneikia explored and blended her interests which lie within the intersections of race, gender, and faith. Following her most recent community and faith organizing work in St. Louis, Missouri, she moved to Atlanta, Georgia, in March 2020 to lend her expertise in facilitating to nonprofit organizations.

Venneikia serves as a committee member for Black Alliance for Peace and Drum Majors Alliance and as a board member for Freedom Arts and Education Center. She also aids the work of Sanctuary Consulting and School of Love. With a bachelors in sociology from UNC-Chapel Hill and a MDiv from Covenant Seminary, Venneikia's womanist lens informs and fuels the work she does: teaching people and organizations how to be active, informed change makers. For the Liberating Church team, Venneikia contributes her unique gifts of communication, marketing, and curriculum development toward the goal of decolonizing Christianity.

TERRANCE HAWKINS

Terrance is a native of Winston-Salem, North Carolina. He is a husband and father and has served locally as a community organizer, speaker, musician, and pastor for the last seventeen years. Terrance is the co-founder of a collective of justice and peace-activists called the Drum Majors Alliance and the founder of a youth development initiative called Lit City. He is also co-executive director of a radical discipleship cohort called School of Love.

WHITNEY WILKINSON ARRECHE

Whitney is a Presbyterian Church (USA) minister who has pastored in Belfast, Northern Ireland, and in rural North Carolina. She is a doctor of theology candidate at Duke University, analyzing how the word *reconciliation* has been used in US Christianity to coerce consent, silence dissent, and further the capitalizing projects of whiteness. She serves as the vice chairperson of the Presbyterian Church (USA) General Assembly Committee for Ecumenical and Interreligious Relations, and on the Faith and Order (Theology) Convening Table of the National Council of Churches. Whitney sees *Liberating Church* as a catalyst for reckoning and truth telling: calling out modern-day plantation churches, and bearing witness to a decolonial Christianity unbeholden to white supremacy. She has written for *The Christian Century* and *Political Theology Network*. She lives in Texas.

JASOLYN HARRIS

Jasolyn is a licensed clinical social worker (LCSW) and MDiv graduate of Duke Divinity School. Jasolyn is also an activist and currently mobilizes with other minoritized students to make Duke Divinity School more equitable, particularly for queer and trans people of color. Prior to returning to school in August of 2016, Jasolyn worked as a sociology instructor at Diablo Valley College, wellness counselor and counseling team supervisor at Aspire Richmond Cal Prep Academy, and academic/general counselor for foster youth at Los Medanos College. Jasolyn also worked at UCSF Benioff Children's Hospital in Oakland, California, as a medical and clinical social worker in the adolescent medicine department and various other places. Jasolyn has extensive experience in crisis, trauma, grief, sexual assault, suicidal/homicidal assessment, and intervention with individuals/communities that hold multiple marginalized identities. As it relates to this project, Jasolyn offers expertise from both her lived and professional experiences as a Black queer woman. Jasolyn is particularly interested in exploring and creating safe, alternative, spiritual spaces for queer and trans people of color who have experienced various amounts of spiritual violence and trauma within Christian churches.

HELMS JARRELL

Helms is a member of the QC Family Tree community in Charlotte, North Carolina, where she and other residents seek to be kinfolk rooted in discipleship in West Charlotte through practices of creativity, prayer, and welcome. QC Family Tree is a community of hospitality and solidarity in a neighborhood that bears the wounds of economic injustice and racial oppression. Helms sees her role in the community as learner, momma, creator, gardener, yogi, pastor, and welcomer. Helms is a graduate of Appalachian State University where she studied communications. She received her MDiv from Baptist Theological Seminary in Richmond, Virginia. Her home church, First Baptist Church, Raleigh, is the church that ordained Helms to ministry in 2003. Helms is also in good standing with the Christian Church (Disciples of Christ). Helms has helped integrate creativity, art, and social practice into the project.

ANTHONY SMITH

Anthony serves as lead pastor of Mission House, a new church start in Salisbury, North Carolina. He is a lead organizer of Rowan Concerned Citizens, a civic engagement group that convenes and facilitates voter education and mobilization initiatives. Anthony is also co-founder and co-chair of the Truth, Healing, Hope and Equity Commission in Salisbury, North Carolina, that is a truth commission patterned after the South African and Greensboro, North Carolina, truth and reconciliation commissions seeking to address systemic inequities in community systems. He is a co-founder of and on the speakers bureau of Transform Network. He has co-authored several books with authors such as Brian McLaren, Sylvia Keesmaat, Shane Claiborne, Elisa Padilla, Richard Twiss et al: *The Justice Project* and *Emergent Manifesto of Hope*. Anthony brings to this team his organic theological and ecclesiological development with his work with Mission House, a church intentionally engaged in embodying a decolonizing Christian faith.

LAURA BYRCH

Laura serves as pastor of community engagement at Boone UMC and as pastor of Blackburn's Chapel in Todd, North Carolina. She is actively involved in local initiatives related to immigrant justice, racial equity, economic and housing justice, food justice, and creating a resilient, trauma-informed community. Laura is passionate about exploring what white accompliceship looks like in her rural context, following the leadership of local leaders of color. She brings to this project a curiosity for how liberating church communities are reshaping our society and transforming faith.

SYMONE WILLIAMS

Symone is currently a final year master's candidate at Yale Divinity School in the Black religion of the African diaspora concentration. Alongside her BA in justice, community, and leadership, professionally, Symone identifies as an advocate, educator, and justice seeker dedicated to forging liberatory practices into everyday actions, and most importantly, centering Black joy. She also runs a small business, Funk & the Sun, where she makes clay earrings by hand while raising mutual aid funds for Black, Indigenous, POC, and queer communities. She has served as a research assistant for the project contributing her skills in graphic design, event planning, data organization, and theological writing.

Bibliography

Baldwin, James. *The Fire Next Time*. New York: Dial, 1963.

———. *The Price of the Ticket: Collected Nonfiction, 1948–1985*. 1st ed. New York: St. Martin's/Marek, 1985.

Berry, Moses. "The Lost Heritage of African-Americans." In *An Unbroken Circle: Linking Ancient African Christianity to the African-American Experience*, edited by Paisius Altschule, 65–73. St. Louis: Brotherhood of St. Moses the Black, 1997.

Boatwright, McHenry. "Steal Away." Track 12 in *The Art of McHenry Boatwright: Spirituals*. Golden Crest Records, 2019.

brown, adrienne marie. *Emergent Strategy: Shaping Change, Changing Worlds*. Chico: AK, 2017.

Cade, John B. "Out of the Mouths of Ex-Slaves." *Journal of Negro History* 20.3 (July 1935) 294–337.

Callahan, Allen Dwight. *The Talking Book: African Americans and the Bible*. New Haven: Yale University Press, 2006.

Chang, Jeff. *Who We Be: The Colorization of America*. New York: St. Martin's, 2014.

Davis, Janae, Alex A Moulton, Levi Van Sant, and Brian Williams. "Anthropocene, Capitalocene, . . . Plantationocene?: A Manifesto for Ecological Justice in an Age of Global Crises." *Geography Compass* 13.5 (2019) 1–15.

Erskine, Noel Leo. *Plantation Church: How African American Religion Was Born in Caribbean Slavery*. Oxford: Oxford University Press, 2014.

Harding, Rachel Elizabeth, and Rosemarie Freeney. *Remnants: A Memoir of Spirit, Activism, and Mothering*. Durham: Duke University Press, 2015.

Harrison, Renee K. *Enslaved Women and the Art of Resistance in Antebellum America*. New York: Palgrave Macmillan, 2009.

Holmes, Barbara A. *Joy Unspeakable: Contemplative Practices of the Black Church*. 2nd ed. Minneapolis: Fortress, 2017.

hooks, bell. *Belonging: A Culture of Place*. New York: Routledge, 2009.

Jackson, Mahalia. "Walk Over God's Heaven." Track 9 in *The World's Greatest Gospel Singer*. Columbia Records, 1955.

BIBLIOGRAPHY

Johnson, James Weldon, J. Rosamond Johnson, and Lawrence Brown. *The Book of American Negro Spirituals*. London: Chapman & Hall, 1926.

Jones, Norrece T., Jr. *Born a Child of Freedom, Yet a Slave: Mechanisms of Control and Strategies of Resistance in Antebellum South Carolina*. Hanover: University Press of New England, 1991.

King, Martin Luther. "A Knock at Midnight." *Stanford University*, June 5, 1963. https://kinginstitute.stanford.edu/king-papers/documents/knock-midnight.

Landis-Aina, Tonetta. "Resistance and Ritual from the Margins: Steal Away." *Resurrection City DC*, November 7, 2021. https://www.resurrectioncitydc.org/media/resistance-ritual-from-the-margins-steal-away.

McKean, Erin. *The New Oxford American Dictionary*. New York: Oxford University Press, 2005.

Myers, Ched. *Binding the Strong Man: A Political Reading of Mark's Story of Jesus*. Maryknoll: Orbis, 1988.

President's Council on Bioethics. *Being Human: Readings from the President's Council on Bioethics*. Washington, DC: President's Council on Bioethics, 2003.

Prower, Tomás. *Queer Magic: LGBT+ Spirituality and Culture from around the World*. Woodbury: Llewellyn Worldwide, Ltd., 2018.

Raboteau, Albert J. *Slave Religion: The "Invisible Institution" in the Antebellum South*. New York: Oxford University Press, 2004.

Rawick, George P. *The American Slave: God Struck Me Dead*. Westport: Greenwood, 1979.

Roy, Arundhati. "The Pandemic Is a Portal." *Financial Times*, April 3, 2020. https://www.ft.com/content/10d8f5e8-74eb-11ea-95fe-fcd274e920ca.

Sampson, Melva L. "Digital Hush Harbors: Black Preaching Women and Black Digital Religious Networks." *Fire!!!* 6.1 (2020) 45–66.

Segundo, Juan Luis. *A Theology for Artisans of a New Humanity, Vol. 1: The Community Called Church*. Translated John Drury. Eugene: Wipf & Stock, 1980.

Sernett, Milton C. *African American Religious History: A Documentary Witness*. Durham: Duke University Press, 1999.

Sharp, Christena. *In the Wake: On Blackness and Being*. Durham: Duke University Press, 2016.

Sweet Honey In The Rock. "Woke Up This Morning with My Mind Stayed on Freedom." Track 2 in *Freedom Song: Television Soundtrack*. Sony BMG Music Entertainment, 2000.

Taylor, Charles. *Modern Social Imaginaries*. Durham: Duke University Press, 2004.

———. *A Secular Age*. London: Belknap, 2007.

Thurman, Howard. *Deep River: Reflections on the Religious Insight of Certain of the Negro Spirituals*. New York: Harper, 1955.

———. *Deep River and the Negro Spiritual Speaks of Life and Death*. Richmond: Friends United, 1975.

————. *Jesus and the Disinherited*. Boston: Beacon, 1996.

Walker, Hezekiah. "I Need You to Survive." Track 7 on *The Essential Hezekiah Walker*. Verity Records/Legacy, 2007.

Walker-Barnes, Chanequa. "Why I Gave Up Church." *Bearings Online*, October 12, 2017. https://collegeville institute.org/bearings/why-i-gave-up-church/.

Lydon, Christopher. "Cornel West on Why James Baldwin Matters More Than Ever." *Literary Hub*, March 2, 2017. https://lithub.com/cornel-west-on-why-james-baldwin-matters-more-than-ever/

Wilson, Cassandra. "Justice." Track 2 on *Belly of the Sun*. Blue Note Records, 2002.

Wilson, Jennie Bain. "Hold to God's Unchanging Hand." In *African American Heritage Hymnal*, no. 404. Chicago: GIA, 2001.

Further Readings and Resources

https://bioethicsarchive.georgetown.edu/pcbe/bookshelf/reader/chapter4.html#introduction

Cade Library Archives: https://subr.libguides.com/c.php?g=413211

https://collegevilleinstitute.org/bearings/why-i-gave-up-church/

https://edgeeffects.net/plantation-legacies-plantationocene/

https://www.thegatheringexperience.com

https://www.goodneighbormovement.org

https://www.liberatingchurch.com

http://missionhousenc.com

https://www.newbirthcommunityame.org

https://www.qcfamilytree.org

Made in the USA
Monee, IL
05 September 2023

42199573R00083